AQA GCSE
Science
Higher Workbook

This book is for anyone doing **AQA GCSE Science** at higher level.

It's full of **tricky questions**........ each one designed to make you **sweat**
— because that's the only way you'll get any **better**.

There are questions to see **what facts** you know. There are questions
to see how well you can **apply those facts**. And there are questions
to see what you know about **how science works**.

It's also got some daft bits in to try and make the whole
experience at least vaguely entertaining for you.

What CGP is all about

Our sole aim here at CGP is to produce the highest
quality books — carefully written, immaculately presented
and dangerously close to being funny.

Then we work our socks off to get them
out to you — at the cheapest possible prices.

Contents

BIOLOGY 1A — HUMAN BIOLOGY

The Nervous System 1
Reflexes 3
Hormones 5
The Menstrual Cycle 6
Controlling Fertility 8
Homeostasis 9
Diet and Exercise 11
Weight Problems 13
Cholesterol and Salt 14
Drugs 16
Alcohol and Tobacco 17
Investigating Drugs 18
Health Claims 21
Fighting Disease 22
Treating Disease — Past and Future 24
Mixed Questions — Biology 1a 26

BIOLOGY 1B — EVOLUTION AND ENVIRONMENT

Adapt and Survive 29
Populations and Competition 31
Variation in Plants and Animals 33
Genes, Chromosomes and DNA 35
Reproduction 36
Cloning 37
Genetic Engineering 38
Evolution 41
Human Impact on the Environment 44
The Greenhouse Effect 46
Climate Change 48
Sustainable Development 49
Mixed Questions — Biology 1b 50

CHEMISTRY 1A — PRODUCTS FROM ROCKS

Atoms and Elements 53
The Periodic Table 54
Compounds and Mixtures 55
Balancing Equations 57
Using Limestone 59
Properties of Metals 63
Metals from Rocks 65
The Reactivity Series 67
Making Metals More Useful 68
More About Metals 70
Fractional Distillation of Crude Oil 71
Properties and Uses of Crude Oil 72
Using Crude Oil as a Fuel 73
Environmental Problems 74
Mixed Questions — Chemistry 1a 77

CHEMISTRY 1B — OILS, EARTH AND ATMOSPHERE

Cracking Crude Oil 81
Alkenes and Ethanol 82
Using Alkenes to Make Polymers 83
Plant Oils and Emulsions 85
Extracting and Using Plant Oils 86
Using Plant Oils 88
Food Additives 89
Plate Tectonics 91
The Earth's Structure 93
The Evolution of the Atmosphere 95
Mixed Questions — Chemistry 1b 99

PHYSICS 1A — ENERGY AND ELECTRICITY

Heat Transfer 102
Heat Radiation 104
Heat Conduction 106
Heat Convection 107
Useful Heat Transfers 109
Energy Transfer 111
Efficiency of Machines 112
Energy Transformations 115
Energy Transformation Diagrams 116
The Cost of Electricity 118
Energy Efficiency in the Home 119
Electricity and the National Grid 121
Non-renewable Energy & Power Stations 122
Using Renewable Energy Resources (1) 123
Using Renewable Energy Resources (2) 124
Using Renewable Energy Resources (3) 126
Using Renewable Energy Resources (4) 127
Comparison of Energy Resources 128
Mixed Questions — Physics 1a 130

PHYSICS 1B — RADIATION AND THE UNIVERSE

Electromagnetic Waves (1) 133
Electromagnetic Waves (2) 134
Microwaves and Infrared 136
Hazards of EM Radiation 140
Analogue and Digital Signals 141
Radioactivity (1) 142
Radioactivity (2) 143
Half-life 145
Uses of Radiation 147
Risks from Radiation 149
The Origin of the Universe 151
Looking into Space 152
Mixed Questions — Physics 1b 154

Published by Coordination Group Publications Ltd.

Editors:
Ellen Bowness, Sarah Hilton, Kate Houghton, Sharon Keeley, Kate Redmond, Ami Snelling.

Contributors:
Antonio Angelosanto, Steve Coggins, Vikki Cunningham, Jane Davies, Ian H. Davis,
Catherine Debley, Philippa Falshaw, James Foster, Anna-fe Guy, Dr Iona MJ Hamilton,
Rebecca Harvey, Frederick Langridge, Barbara Mascetti, Lucy Muncaster,
Sidney Stringer Community School, Paul Warren, Andy Williams, Dee Wyatt.

ISBN-10: 1 84146 706 5
ISBN-13: 978 1 84146 706 1

*With thanks to Vanessa Aris, Barrie Crowther, Ian Francis and Glenn Rogers for the proofreading.
With thanks to Katie Steele for the copyright research.*

Data used to construct the graph on page 25 provided by the Health Protection Agency.

*Graph of sulfur dioxide emissions on page 44 compiled by NETCEN on behalf of the
Department of the Environment, Food and Rural Affairs.*

*Graph of average surface temperature of Earth on page 47 © Crown copyright 1995,
Published by the Met Office.*

*With thanks to the Intergovernmental Panel on Climate Change for permission to reproduce
the graph of atmospheric gas concentrations used on page 47.*

*With thanks to East Midlands Aggregate Working Party/National Stone Centre for permission
to reproduce the data used on page 60.*

Groovy website: www.cgpbooks.co.uk

Printed by Elanders Hindson Ltd, Newcastle upon Tyne.
Jolly bits of clipart from CorelDRAW®

The Nervous System

Q1 Complete the following passage by choosing the correct words from the box.

organs	motor	effectors	neurones	sensory	glands	electrical

Nerve cells or .... transmit .... impulses from our sense organs to

the CNS. Messages from the CNS are sent to ...., which are muscles or

.... The impulses are carried along .... and .... neurones.

Q2 Which of the following is **not** an example of a **stimulus**? Underline your answer.

pressure   chemical   hearing   change in body position   change in temperature

Q3 In each sentence below, underline the **sense organ** involved and write down the **type of receptor** that is detecting the stimulus.

a) Tariq puts a piece of lemon on his tongue. The lemon tastes sour.

....

b) Siobhan wrinkles her nose as she smells something unpleasant in her baby brother's nappy.

....

c) Lindsey covers her eyes when she sees the man in the mask jump out during a scary film.

....

d) Xabi's ears were filled with the sound of the crowd cheering his outstanding goal.

....

Q4 Give two reasons why it is important for animals to be able to **detect changes** in their surroundings.

....

....

....

Q5 Explain why a man with a damaged spinal cord may not be able to feel someone touching his toe.

....

....

....

The Nervous System

Q6 Some parts of the body are known as the CNS.

a) What do the letters **CNS** stand for? ....

b) Name the two main parts of the CNS.

1. .... 2. ....

c) What type of neurone:

i) carries information to the CNS? ....

ii) carries instructions from the CNS? ....

Q7 John and Marc investigated how **sensitive** different parts of the body are to **pressure**.
They stuck two pins in a cork 0.5 cm apart. The pins were placed on different parts of the body.
Ten pupils took part — they were blindfolded and reported "yes" or "no" to feeling both points.
The results of the experiment are shown in the table.

Area of the body tested	Number of pupils reporting 'yes'
Sole of foot	2
Knee	3
Fingertip	10
Back of hand	5
Lip	9

a) Which part of the body do the results suggest is:

i) most sensitive? .... **ii)** least sensitive ....

b) From the results above, which part of the body do you think
contains the **most pressure receptors**? Explain your answer.

....

....

c) John and Marc took it in turns to test the pupils. Their teacher suggested that if only one of
the boys had done all the testing, the experiment would have been fairer. Explain why.

....

....

d) Each pupil was tested once. Suggest how you might make the test more accurate.

....

....

Reflexes

Q1 Circle the correct answer to complete each of the following sentences.

a) Reflexes happen more **quickly** / **slowly** than considered responses.

b) The **vertebrae** / **spinal cord** can coordinate a reflex response.

c) The main purpose of a reflex is to **protect** / **display** the body.

d) Reflexes happen **with** / **without** you thinking about them.

e) A synapse is a connection between two **effectors** / **neurones**.

Q2 Look carefully at the diagrams showing two different eyes below.

Eye A

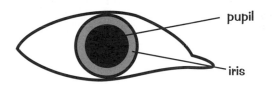

Eye B

— pupil

— iris

a) Describe the difference you can see in the appearance of the two eyes.

....

....

b) Which diagram do you think shows an eye in bright light? Explain your answer.

....

....

....

c) Is the response illustrated by the diagrams above a considered response or a reflex response?

....

d) Explain why it is an advantage to have this type of response controlling the action of the eye.

....

....

....

Reflexes

Q3 Why is a **reflex** reaction faster than a **voluntary** reaction?

> Think about where the impulse has to go to.

....

....

Q4 Explain what a **reflex arc** is.

....

....

Q5 When you touch something hot with a finger you **automatically** pull the finger away. The diagram shows some parts of the nervous system involved in this **reflex action**.

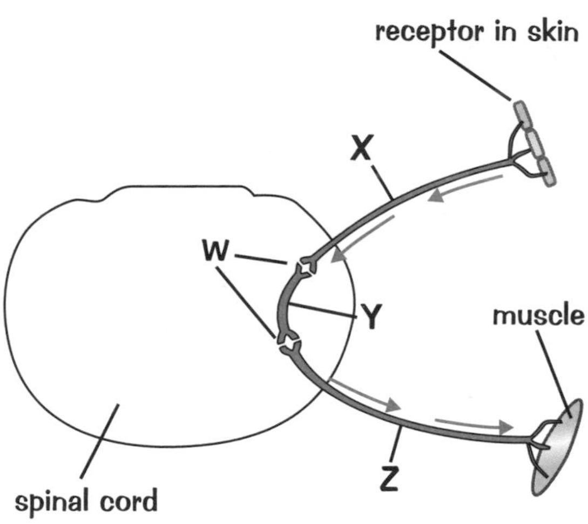

receptor in skin

X

W

Y

muscle

Z

spinal cord

a) What type of neurone is:

i) neurone **X**? ....

ii) neurone **Y**? ....

iii) neurone **Z**? ....

b) In what form is the information carried:

i) along neurone **X**?

....

ii) from neurone **X** to neurone **Y**?

....

c) Complete the sentence.

In this reflex action the muscle acts as the ....

d) i) What are the gaps marked **W** on the diagram called? ....

ii) Explain how the impulse get across these gaps.

....

....

....

Top Tips: Reflexes are really fast — that's the whole point of them. And the fewer synapses the signals have to cross, the faster the reaction. Doctors test people's reflexes by tapping below their knees to make their legs jerk. This reflex takes less than 50 milliseconds as only two synapses are involved.

Hormones

Q1 Complete the passage below about **hormones**.

> Hormones are .... messengers. They are produced in
> .... and released into the ....
> They are carried all around the body, but only affect certain .... cells.

Q2 What is the '**fight or flight**' hormone? Why is it known in this way?

....

....

Q3 Fit the answers to the clues into the grid.

   a) Gland that produces insulin

   b) Hormone produced by the pituitary

   c) Insulin controls the level of this in the blood

   d) Transports hormones around the body

   e) Hormone produced by the testes

Q4 Describe the major differences between responses brought about by **hormones** and those due to the **nervous system**.

....

....

....

Q5 ADH is a hormone which causes the kidneys to remove less water from the blood.

   a) Name gland X. ....

   b) Suggest what triggers gland X to produce ADH.

   ....

   ....

6

The Menstrual Cycle

Q1 FSH has two functions in the menstrual cycle.

a) What are these functions?

1. ....

2. ....

b) What effect does oestrogen have on the production of FSH?

....

Q2 Answer the following questions about **LH**.

a) What does LH stand for?

....

b) What causes LH to be released?

....

c) When does the LH cause the release of an egg from the ovary?

....

Q3 There are three main **hormones** involved in the menstrual cycle.

a) Complete the table to show **where** in the body each hormone is produced.

HORMONE	WHERE IT IS PRODUCED
FSH	
oestrogen	
LH	

b) Give two effects that oestrogen has in the body of an adult woman.

1. ....

2. ....

Top Tips: Sometimes, it's haaard to be... a womaaan... Or a man for that matter, if you're trying to learn about the menstrual cycle. This isn't really a topic where your natural intelligence and deep understanding of science can shine through much — you've just got to get your head down and learn the four stages and what each hormone does. Sorry.

Biology 1a — Human Biology

The Menstrual Cycle

Q4 These diagrams show some events in the **menstrual cycle**. Put the events in the order they happen in the menstrual cycle by writing numbers in the boxes, then describe each event **briefly**.

Don't forget, the cycle begins with the first day of a period.

☐ ....
....

☐ ....
....

☐ ....
....

Don't forget, 'uterus' is just the biological word for the 'womb'.

Q5 An **egg** is usually released on day 14 of the menstrual cycle.

a) Why does the uterus wall become thick and spongy before the egg is released?

....

....

b) Explain why there are only a few days in each menstrual cycle when fertilisation can take place.

....

....

c) What happens in the uterus if the egg is not fertilised?

....

<u>*Controlling Fertility*</u>

Q1   Hormones can be used to **increase fertility**.

a)   Name the hormone that is often given to women who are not releasing any eggs.

....

b)   The passage below explains how this hormone works.
Use the words in the box to fill in the gaps. Each word should be used once.

| pituitary gland | LH | egg | FSH | ovary | oestrogen |

.... stimulates the ovaries to produce .... ,

which stimulates the .... to produce ....

This stimulates the .... to release an ....

Q2   Using hormones to increase or reduce fertility in women has some **disadvantages**.
Complete the table below to show some of the disadvantages of taking hormones.

Use	Possible disadvantages
Reducing fertility	**1.** ....
	2. ....
Increasing fertility	**1.** ....
	2. ....

Q3   **The pill** is an **oral contraceptive** that contains oestrogen. Explain how it is used to reduce fertility.

....

....

Q4   **In vitro fertilisation** can help couples to have children.

a)   Explain how **in vitro fertilisation** works.

....

....

....

b)   Discuss the advantages and disadvantages of in vitro fertilisation.

....

....

....

Homeostasis

Q1   Define **homeostasis**.

....

....

Q2   The human body is usually maintained at a temperature of about **37 °C**.

a)   Why do humans suffer ill effects if their body temperature varies too much from this temperature?

....

....

b)   Which part of your body monitors your body temperature to ensure that it is kept constant?

....

c)   How does your body cool down when it is too hot?

....

Q3   The graph shows the **blood sugar levels** of a healthy person over a period of 5 hours.

a)   What might have caused the drop in blood sugar level at point A?

....

b)   The blood sugar level rose quickly at point B. What could have caused this increase in sugar level?

....

c) i)   Which hormone caused the blood sugar to return to normal at point C?

....

ii)   Where in the body is this hormone produced? Underline the correct answer below.

The pituitary gland   **The kidneys**

The muscles   **The pancreas**

Homeostasis

Q4 Choose the correct words to complete the paragraph below.

On a **cold** / **hot** day or when you're exercising, you **sweat a lot** / **don't sweat much**, so

you will produce **more** / **less** urine. The urine will be a **pale** / **dark** colour as it contains

less / **more** water than usual. We say that the urine is more **concentrated** / **dilute** than usual.

Q5 Ronald eats a meal that is very high in **salt**. Which of the answers below explain correctly how Ronald's body gets rid of this excess salt? Tick one or more boxes.

☐ Ronald's liver removes salt from his blood.

☐ Ronald loses salt in his sweat.

☐ Ronald's kidneys remove salt from his blood.

☐ Ronald's saliva becomes more salty, and the salt is lost when he breathes.

☐ Ronald gets rid of salt in his urine.

Q6 The Big Brother contestants are getting on my nerves, so I put each of them on a treadmill and turn the setting to high (just to keep them quiet for a bit).

Will the contestants lose **more** or **less** water from the following body parts than they would if they sat still? Explain your answers.

a) Skin ....

....

b) Lungs ....

....

c) Kidneys ....

....

Q7 Mrs Finnegan had the **concentration of ions** in her urine measured on two days.

Date	6th December	20th July
Average air temperature	8 °C	24 °C
Ion concentration in urine	1.5 mg/cm³	2.1 mg/cm³

Assuming Mrs Finnegan always eats exactly the same food every day, suggest a reason for the different ion concentrations in her urine.

....

....

Diet and Exercise

Q1   The bar chart shows the proportions of each **food group** that make up three different foods.

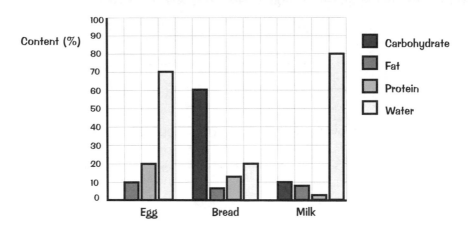

a)   Which food contains the highest proportion of fat? ....

b)   What is the difference between the amount of carbohydrate in 50 g of bread and the amount of carbohydrate in 50 g of milk? Give your answer in grams and show your working out.

....

....

The % in the bar chart is like the no. of grams you'd have in 100 g of the food.

c)   For my lunch I have scrambled eggs on toast and a glass of milk. Suggest another food I could have to make this a more balanced meal. Explain your answer.

....

....

Q2   Different people need to eat **different amounts** of food because they have different energy requirements.

Calories are a measure of the amount of energy in food.

a)   It is recommended that the average woman eats about 2000 Calories per day, while the average man should eat about 2500 Calories. Explain why there is a difference.

....

....

b)   Cyclists riding in the Tour de France bike race need to eat about 6000 Calories per day during the race. This is more than twice what the average man requires. Explain why.

....

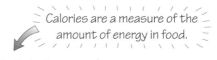

....

Top Tips: Mmm, what I couldn't do with 6000 Calories per day... Anyway, remember that everyone needs a balanced diet, but not everyone needs to eat exactly the same stuff. The amount you need depends on your metabolic rate and how much exercise you do — more on this on the next page.

Biology 1a — Human Biology

Diet and Exercise

Q3 Answer the following questions about **metabolism**.

a) What is meant by 'metabolic rate'?

....

....

b) What effect does being overweight have on your metabolic rate? Explain your answer.

....

....

c) How would taking up regular exercise affect your resting metabolic rate? Explain your answer.

....

....

Q4 Explain why you need less energy from your diet if you live in a hot climate.

....

....

Q5 Complete the following sentences to show the functions in the body of different food groups.

a) Protein is needed for .... and ....

b) Carbohydrates provide much of your ....

c) Fats are needed to .... and for ....

d) Fibre keeps your .... working smoothly.

e) Vitamins and minerals are needed in .... amounts to stay healthy.

Q6 How can a person be both 'fit' and **malnourished**?

....

....

Weight Problems

Q1 Lack of food is often a problem in developing countries.

  a) Write down two common effects of malnutrition.

  ....

  b) Children tend to be particularly badly affected when there is a shortage of food. Suggest why.

  ....

Q2 Explain why it can be difficult for researchers to collect **accurate data** on:

  a) malnutrition and starvation. ....

  ....

  ....

  b) obesity. ....

  ....

  ....

Q3 Fifty men and fifty women were asked whether they thought they were **obese**.
  Each was then given a medical examination to **check** whether they were actually obese.

	Thought they were obese	Actually obese
No. of women	9	16
No. of men	5	11

  a) What percentage of women in this survey were obese? ....

  b) What are the most common causes of obesity in developed countries?

  ....

  c) Is an obesity study based on data from questionnaires likely to be accurate?
       Explain your answer.

  ....

  ....

  d) Underline any health problems in the list below that have been linked to obesity.

  heart disease   **hepatitis**   **influenza**   **cancers**   **scurvy**   **diabetes**

Q4 Explain how high levels of obesity could cause **economic problems** in a country like the UK.

  ....

  ....

Cholesterol and Salt

Q1 There are several **risk factors** for heart disease.

a) What is meant by a 'risk factor' for heart disease?

....

b) How does a high level of salt in your diet affect your body?

....

Q2 It is recommended that adults should eat no more than **6 g** of salt each day.

a) Your friend tells you that there is no way that she can be eating
too much salt as she never sprinkles any on her food. Is she right?

....

....

b) The salt in food is usually listed as sodium in the nutritional information on the label.
You can work out the amount of salt using the formula: **salt = sodium × 2.5**

It says there is **0.5 g of sodium per serving** of soup. How much salt is this?

....

....

Q3 This question is about **lipoproteins**.

a) What are lipoproteins?

....

b) Name the two types of lipoproteins involved in the transport of cholesterol in the blood.

....

c) Explain what is meant by 'bad cholesterol' and 'good cholesterol'.

....

....

....

Q4 Name the three main types of fat found in our diet and say how their **carbon chains** differ.

....

....

....

Cholesterol and Salt

Q5   In a minor **heart attack** the flow of blood in the heart muscle is reduced.

a)   Explain how too much cholesterol can lead to this type of heart attack.

....

....

b)   Which organ controls the level of cholesterol in the body?

....

Q6   The following table shows the **fat content** of two different butter substitute spreads.

TYPE OF FAT	PERCENTAGE IN SPREAD A	PERCENTAGE IN SPREAD B
Saturated	10	50
Monounsaturated	35	31
Polyunsaturated	54	15
Trans fatty acids	1	4

a)   Complete the pie charts to show this information.

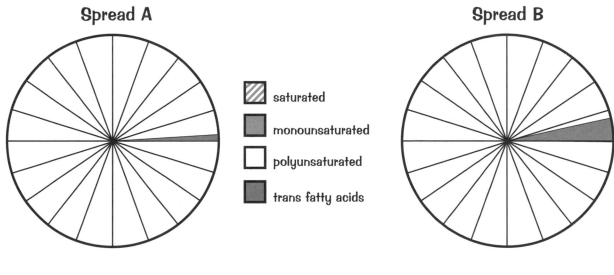

b)   The packaging of one of the spreads says it is 'proven to reduce cholesterol levels'. Which spread do you think this is? Explain your answer.

....

....

Top Tips: Mmm, I just fancy a plate of chips now... It's a bit depressing, all this 'risk factor', 'bad cholesterol' talk, isn't it? But don't be scared — just about everything is bad for you if you do it too much. Even chips are OK in moderation — just don't have them every day.

<u>Drugs</u>

Q1 a) What does the term 'drug' mean?

....

b) What does it mean if you are **addicted** to a drug?

....

....

Q2 Write numbers in the boxes below to show the correct **order** in which drugs are tested.

☐ Drug is tested on human tissue.　　☐ Computer models simulate a response to the drug.

　　☐ Human volunteers are used to test the drug.　　☐ Drug is tested on live animals.

Q3 Before drugs are made freely available, **clinical trials** must be performed.

a) What is a 'clinical trial'?

....

b) Give two reasons why clinical trials have to be done before drugs are made freely available.

....

....

c) Explain why clinical trials can't be done on human tissue samples only.

....

....

Q4 **Thalidomide** is a drug that was developed in the 1950s.

a) What was this drug originally developed for?

....

b) Thalidomide was not fully tested. What effect did it have when given to pregnant women?

....

....

c) Why has this drug been reintroduced recently?

....

Q5 Outline the arguments for and against using **live animals** for testing new drugs.

....

....

....

Alcohol and Tobacco

Q1 In the UK, the legal limit for alcohol in the blood when driving is **80 mg per 100 cm³**. The table shows the number of 'units' of alcohol in different drinks. One **unit** increases the blood alcohol level by over **20 mg per 100 cm³** in most people.

DRINK	ALCOHOL UNITS
1 pint of strong lager	3
1 pint of beer	2
1 single measure of whisky	1

a) Bill drinks two pints of strong lager. How many units of alcohol has he had? ....

b) Is Bill's blood alcohol level likely to mean that he cannot legally drive? Explain your answer.

....

....

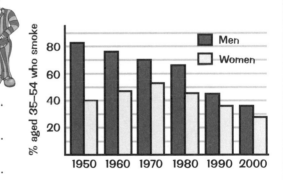
Assume he drank the cans fairly quickly.

c) Explain why it can be dangerous to drive a car after drinking alcohol.

....

Q2 a) Alcohol can cause **dehydration**. What effect does this have on the brain?

....

b) Which other organ is often damaged by excessive alcohol intake? ....

Q3 The graph shows how the number of **smokers** aged between 35 and 54 in the UK has changed since 1950.

a) Describe the main trends you can see in this graph.

....

....

....

....

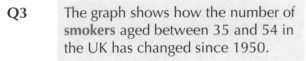

b) Why are smokers more likely to suffer from:

i) chest infections ....

....

ii) cancers ....

Q4 a) Why do alcohol and smoking have a **bigger impact** than illegal drugs in the UK?

....

b) Give two ways in which misuse of alcohol and smoking **negatively** affect the **economy** in the UK.

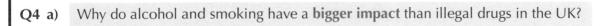

....

....

Investigating Drugs

Q1 Smoking is now known to be dangerous and many people try to give up. People often find this **difficult** so there are products and methods to help them. These include **hypnosis, acupuncture** and **nicotine replacement** using patches or gums.

a) Why is it hard to give up smoking?

....

b) Which of the methods listed above is supported most by scientific evidence?

....

c) Explain how nicotine gum may help someone to give up.

....

....

Q2 Decide which of these statements are **facts** and which are **opinions**.
Write '**F**' for fact or '**O**' for opinion in each box.

☐ Crack cocaine is highly addictive.   ☐ Soft drugs are safe to use.

☐ Using cannabis relaxes you.   ☐ Heroin can relieve pain.

☐ Only people with addictive personalities become addicts.

Q3 There are three main opinions about the **link** between cannabis and hard drugs.
Explain the idea behind each of the following:

a) Stepping stone: ....

b) Gateway drug: ....

c) Genetics: ....

Q4 In the early 20th century, the number of people developing **lung cancer** was
increasing. At the same time it was noted that more people were **smoking**.

a) Give **three** possible explanations for the correlation between lung cancer and smoking.

1. ....

2. ....

3. ....

b) Which of your explanations do you think cigarette manufacturers favoured? Explain your answer.

....

....

Investigating Drugs

Q5   Read the article below and answer the questions that follow.

In the UK, all illegal drugs belong to one of three classes — A, B or C — depending on how harmful they are. The punishments for possessing (or dealing) class A drugs are more severe than for class C drugs.

In January 2004, cannabis was 'reclassified' as a class C drug. Previously, it had been in class B, along with amphetamines like 'speed'. The Government decided to 'downgrade' cannabis because most evidence showed that it was less harmful than the other class B drugs.

There's still a lot of debate about how harmful cannabis is, though. Many people are worried that cannabis is linked to mental illnesses like depression and schizophrenia.

 In one study, scientists monitored the mental health of about 1600 teenagers at 44 different schools in Australia, over a seven-year period.

They found that girls who used cannabis every day were five times more likely to suffer from depression by the age of 20. Those who used cannabis less frequently (but at least once a week) were twice as likely to suffer from depression as non-users.

Another team of scientists studied a group of older men in Sweden. Their study involved 50 000 men who did their compulsory military service between 1969 and 1970. When they began military service (aged 18–20), these men all gave details about how often they used cannabis (and other drugs). The researchers then examined the men's medical records from 1970 to 1996, to see how many of them suffered from schizophrenia in later life. They found that the more frequently a person used cannabis, the more likely they were to develop schizophrenia.

> Remember that the independent variable is the one that is changed, and the dependent variable is the one that is measured.

a)   The following questions are about the **Swedish** study.

i)   What were the dependent and independent variables in this study?

Dependent variable: ....

Independent variable: ....

ii) Drug use was measured by asking the men how often they used drugs.
What is the main problem with this kind of '**self-reporting**'?

....

....

b)   Fill in the information below about the **Australian** study.

Sample size: ....

Time period covered: ....

Independent variable: ....

Dependent variable: ....

Investigating Drugs

c) **i)** Write 'true' or 'false' next to each of the statements below.

   A Cannabis was legalised in 2004. ....

   B Punishments for dealing class A drugs are harsher than for dealing class C drugs. ....

   C Amphetamines are class C drugs. ....

   D Most evidence suggests that cannabis is more harmful than class A drugs. ....

   ii) Write correct versions of the statements above that are **false**.

   ....

   ....

   ....

d) The **Australian** study looked at cannabis use amongst teenage girls.

   i) Complete the bar chart of the results.

   Read over the passage again if you're not sure. Remember, the bar chart gives you the level for those girls who never used cannabis.

   Number of girls suffering from depression after different frequencies of cannabis use

   (bar chart: y-axis "Number of girls suffering from depression"; x-axis "Frequency of cannabis use" with categories daily, at least weekly, never)

   ii) What link is suggested by this study?

   ....

   ....

   ....

   iii) Do these results **prove** that cannabis use causes depression? Explain your answer.

   ....

   ....

   ....

e) Which of the two studies do you think provides the most **reliable** results, and why?

   ....

   ....

   ....

Top Tips: So, after all that time, effort and money, the answer is ...erm, we dunno. Maybe it causes mental health problems, and then again, maybe it doesn't. That's science for you. There could be **another factor** that makes people more likely to take drugs **and** more likely to become mentally ill.

Health Claims

Q1 Scientists are still **not sure** whether there is a link between using cannabis and developing mental health problems, despite the fact that lots of studies have been carried out. Explain why this is.

....

....

Q2 Two reports on **low-fat foods** were published on one day. **Report A** appeared in a tabloid paper. It said that the manufacturers of 'Crunchie Bites' have shown that the latest girl band, Kandyfloss, lost weight using their product. **Report B** appeared in the *Journal of Medicine* and reported how 6000 volunteers lost weight during a trial of an experimental medicine.

Which of these reports is likely to be the most reliable and why?

....

....

Q3 Three **weight loss methods** appeared in the headlines last week.

① **Hollywood star swears carrot soup aids weight loss**

② **Survey of 10 000 dieters shows it's exercise that counts**

③ **Atkins works! 5000 in study lose weight... but what about their health?**

a) Which of these headlines are more likely to refer to **scientific studies**? Explain your answer.

....

....

b) Why might following the latest celebrity diet not always help you lose weight?

....

....

Q4 A drug trial involved 6000 patients with **high cholesterol levels**. 3000 patients were given **statins**, and 3000 were not. Both were advised to make lifestyle changes to lower their cholesterol. The decrease in their cholesterol levels compared to their levels at the start is shown on the graph.

a) Why was the group without statin included?

....

b) Suggest a conclusion that can be drawn from these results. ....

....

Fighting Disease

Q1   Fill in the gaps in the passage below using the words in the box.

cells	bursts	celled	DNA	damaging	toxins	damage	copies

Bacteria are single-.............................. organisms which can multiply rapidly. Some can

make you ill by .... your body cells or producing ....

Viruses are tiny particles — they are not .... They are often made up of

a coat of protein and a strand of .... Viruses replicate by fooling body cells

into making .... of them. The cell then .... and releases

the new virus. This cell .... makes you feel ill.

Q2   If a person has an organ transplant, they may have to take drugs to **suppress** their immune system and stop the organ being **rejected**. Why is it important that these people **avoid infection**?

....

....

Q3   **White blood cells** protect the body from infection.

a)   Give **three** ways that they do this.

....

....

....

b)   How do white blood cells recognise particular types of pathogen?

....

c)   Explain what **natural immunity** is.

....

....

....

d)   How does the body try to protect itself from infection through cuts?

....

....

Fighting Disease

Q4   Define these terms.

a)   pathogen: ....

b)   immunisation: ....

c)   antigens: ....

d)   booster: ....

Q5   A new medicine called 'Killcold' contains **painkillers** and **decongestants**.

a)   Explain why its name isn't strictly accurate.

....

....

b)   Why don't doctors give antibiotics for colds?

....

....

c)   Why is it more difficult to develop drugs to destroy viruses than it is to develop drugs to kill bacteria?

Think about where in the body viruses like to hang out so that they can replicate themselves.

....

....

Q6   John gets injected with the **rubella vaccine** but James doesn't. Soon afterwards both boys are exposed to the rubella virus. Explain why James gets ill but John **doesn't**.

....

....

....

Q7   Jay is given **antibiotics** for an infection. Soon he feels better, so he doesn't finish the full course of antibiotics. How may this lead to the development of **antibiotic-resistant strains** of bacteria?

....

....

....

Top Tips: Pathogens arc all nasty little blighters that make you ill if they manage to get inside you. Bacteria and viruses are both pathogens but they have totally different structures and methods of attack — make sure you know the differences. And remember — antibiotics kill bacteria, not viruses.

Treating Disease — Past and Future

Q1 Answer the questions below about **immunisation**.

a) Describe how immunisations have changed the pattern of disease in the UK.

....

....

b) Name a disease that has been **eradicated** worldwide because of immunisation programmes.

....

c) Describe **two** problems that occasionally occur with vaccines.

....

....

Q2 The MMR vaccine protects against measles, mumps and rubella. There is a small risk that children will suffer serious side effects to the vaccine such as meningitis or convulsions. However, the Government recommends that **all** children are given the MMR vaccine. Explain why this is.

....

....

....

Q3 Ignaz Semmelweiss worked in a hospital in Vienna in the 1840s. The graph shows the percentage of women dying after childbirth, before and after a **change** that he made.

a) What was the change and why did it help?

....

....

....

b) After Semmelweiss left, the doctors went back to their old ways. Why do you think this was?

....

....

Treating Disease — Past and Future

Q4 The graph shows the number of people catching **measles**, and the number being **immunised** against it in the UK.

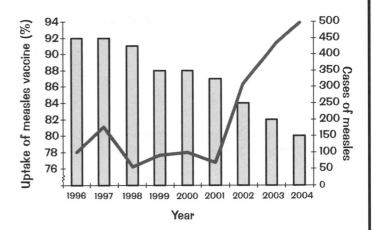

☐ Uptake of measles vaccine (%)

— Cases of measles

*Number of cases of measles includes those confirmed by testing serum & by oral fluid.

a) What happened to the number of people catching measles as the number being immunised decreased over the time period shown on the graph?

....

b) The graph appears to show a **threshold level** of immunisation. When the percentage of people being immunised falls **below** this threshold level, the number of measles cases starts increasing. What is this threshold level?

....

c) The **more** people there are in the population that **have** been immunised against measles, the **less likely** you are to catch it, even if you yourself have **not** been immunised. Explain why.

....

....

Q5 Some bacteria and viruses **evolve quickly**.

a) Why is rapid **bacterial** evolution such a threat to human health?

....

....

b) It can be difficult to find an effective **vaccine** against diseases caused by pathogens that evolve rapidly. Explain why.

....

....

....

Top Tips:

Of course, Darwin was right when he said that evolution happens gradually over many generations. The trouble is, with bacteria and viruses, a whole generation can take about ten minutes. Hmmm.

Mixed Questions — Biology 1a

Q1 The diagram shows a runner waiting to start a race in the Olympic Games.

a) Give one sense organ that the athlete is relying on at the start of the race, and state the type of receptors it uses.

....

b) When the athlete starts the race, information will travel around his body via neurones.
   i) What is the difference between motor neurones and sensory neurones?

....

   ii) Explain how a nerve signal passes from one neurone to the next.

....

....

c) Some information is sent around the body using hormones rather than nervous impulses.

   i) How do hormones travel around the body?

....

   ii) Describe **three** differences in the way nerves and hormones work in the body.

....

....

....

Q2 The diagram represents the **menstrual cycle** in a particular woman.

a) What is the length of the complete menstrual cycle shown?

.... days.

b) What happens on day 16 of this woman's cycle?

....

c) Oestrogen is one of the main hormones that control the menstrual cycle. What other role does oestrogen have in the female body?

....

d) Explain how the oestrogen in the contraceptive pill prevents pregnancy.

....

....

Mixed Questions — Biology 1a

Q3 a) Complete the passage below by choosing the correct words to fill in the gaps.

saturated	salt	HDL	LDL	hypertension	polyunsaturated	scurvy	liver

The amount of cholesterol in the blood is controlled by the ....
Cholesterol is transported around the body by two kinds of lipoprotein. One is known as 'good
cholesterol' or .... The other form is ...., and is
sometimes called 'bad cholesterol'. Eating more .... fats can improve the
balance between good and bad cholesterol.

b) A high 'bad' cholesterol level puts you at risk of heart disease.
Give two factors linked to **diet** that also affect your chances of getting heart disease.

....

Q4 a) Circle the best word or phrase from each pair to complete the sentences below.

i) **Carbohydrates** / **Vitamins** are needed in tiny amounts to keep you healthy.

ii) Obesity tends to be a problem in **developed** / **developing** countries.

iii) An overweight person usually has a **higher** / **lower** metabolic rate than an average person.

iv) A farmer is likely to need a lot **more** / **less** energy than someone working in a call centre.

v) Carbohydrates are broken down into sugars to provide **energy** / **materials to build new cells**.

b) Water is a vital part of our diet and the body's water level is controlled by homeostasis.

i) Name three ways that water is lost from the body.

....

ii) Explain why the amount of urine that people produce can depend on the air temperature.

....

....

Q5 Scientists spend a lot of time **researching** new diets and drugs.

a) Why are drugs tested on animals before they are used in clinical trials?

....

b) List three factors that can give you an indication of how reliable a scientific report is.

....

....

Mixed Questions — Biology 1a

Q6   Tick the boxes below that are next to **true** statements.

It is now widely accepted that smoking increases the risk of lung cancer.

Alcohol doesn't tend to cause serious problems because it is legal.

It is now widely accepted that using cannabis increases the risk of mental health problems.

Until more scientific evidence is available, scientists can't be sure that smoking is harmful.

Some studies have found a link between cannabis use and mental health problems.

It has been proven that the desire to take cannabis and other drugs is genetic.

Q7   Gavin and Van carried out an experiment at school to investigate the effectiveness of six different **antibiotics** (1–6). They spread some bacteria onto a sterile agar plate. They then placed discs of filter paper, impregnated with the six different antibiotics, onto the bacterial culture.

a)   Define the term "antibiotic".

....

b)   Explain what has happened in the "clear zone" labelled on the diagram.

....

c)   Which of the antibiotics (1–6) was the most effective against these bacteria? ....

d)   Would these antibiotics also work against the flu? Explain your answer.

....

e)   Why do doctors prescribe antibiotics as infrequently as possible?

....

....

f)   Fortunately, many people with infections don't need antibiotics because their bodies have ways of dealing with pathogens. Explain how some white blood cells use antibodies to kill bacteria.

....

....

g)   Why are people vaccinated against diseases such as mumps even though their white blood cells are able to fight the pathogens?

....

Adapt and Survive

Q1   Pictures of a **polar bear** and a small rodent called a **kangaroo rat** are shown below.

Diagrams are
not to scale.

a)   Which of these animals do you think has the smallest body surface area? ....

b)   Which animal has the smallest body
surface area **compared to its volume**? ....

This is a tricky one. Remember, long, thin shapes have a big surface area compared to their volume.

c)   Explain how this animal's **shape** helps to reduce its
body surface area compared to its volume.

....

d)   Does having a **smaller** body surface area compared to volume mean that more or less **heat** can be
lost from an animal's body?

....

e)   The kangaroo rat lives in hot desert regions. Would you expect its body surface area compared to
volume to be bigger or smaller than the polar bear's? Explain why.

....

....

....

Q2   The picture shows a **cactus** plant.

a)   Where are cactus plants usually found? Underline the correct answer below.

In Arctic regions   In the desert   In the mountains   Near the sea

b)   Explain how each of the following parts of the cactus help it to survive in its normal habitat.

i) Spines ....

....

ii) Stem ....

....

iii) Roots ....

....

Adapt and Survive

Q3   Complete the passage using the words given. Each can be used more than once or not at all.

heat concentrated sweat water large offspring small night dilute
Mammals living in deserts need to conserve .... They make .... amounts of very .... urine. They also produce very little .... They keep cool in other ways, e.g. by only coming out at ....

Q4   The picture shows two different types of fox.

Fox A

Fox B

a)   State two differences in the appearance of the foxes.

1. ....

2. ....

b)   Identify which fox lives in a cold Arctic region and which lives in a desert.

i) Fox A ....   **ii)** Fox B ....

c)   Explain how the features you described in part a) help each fox to survive in its natural habitat.

1. ....

....

2. ....

....

Q5   Hayley measured some cubes to find out their surface area to volume ratio. Her results are shown in the table.

Length of cube side (cm)	Surface area of cube (cm²)	Volume of cube (cm²)	Surface area: volume ratio
2	24	8	
4	96	64	
6	216	216	
8	384	512	
10	600	1000	

a)   Calculate the **surface area : volume ratio** for each cube and write your answers in the table.

Just divide the surface area by the volume.

b)   As the cube size becomes larger, what happens to the value of the **surface area : volume ratio**?

....

c)   Would you expect the smallest cube (length 2 cm) or the largest cube (length 10 cm) to lose heat more quickly? Explain your answer.

....

d)   Use your answers above to explain why a mouse has a thick covering of fur.

....

....

Biology 1b — Evolution and Environment

Populations and Competition

Q1 Indicate whether each behaviour involves animals trying to compete (**C**) or acting as predators (**P**) by putting a cross in the correct column.

BEHAVIOUR	C	P
Stags grow antlers during the mating season		
A pack of wolves work together to kill a moose		
A magpie chases a sparrow away from a bird-table		
Spiders spin webs to trap flies		
Lions chase leopards and cheetahs from their territory		

Q2 **Algae** are tiny plants that are eaten by **fish**. The graph shows how the size of a population of algae in a pond varied throughout one year.

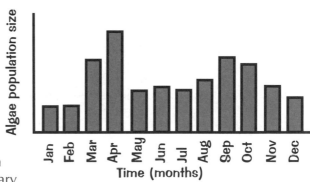

a) Suggest two conditions that may have changed in the pond to give more algae in April than in January.

....

b) The number of **fish** in the pond increased rapidly during one month of the year. Suggest which month this was. Explain your answer.

....

....

Q3 Jenny cultured some bacteria in a Petri dish. She counted the number of colonies (clumps of cells) at intervals as they spread across the dish. Her results are shown in the table.

Time (minutes)	No. of bacterial colonies
0	1
20	2
40	4
60	8
80	16
100	32
120	64

a) Suggest two things Jenny had to provide the bacteria with to allow them to grow.

1) ....   2) ....

b) Calculate the number of bacterial colonies you would expect to find after 3 hours.

....

Hint: look for a pattern in Jenny's results and continue it.

c) After 3 hours, Jenny found that the number of bacterial colonies stopped increasing. Suggest why this might be.

....

....

Populations and Competition

Q4   The table shows how the UK's barn owl population has changed over a period of 20 years.

Year	No. of barn owl pairs (thousands)
1970	7
1980	4.5
1990	1.4

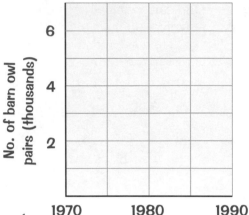

a)   Use the table to plot a graph showing the change in the size of the barn owl population over time. Use the grid provided.

b)   Estimate the population size in 1985. ....

c)   Suggest **two** reasons why the barn owl population has decreased in recent years.

....

....

Q5   The graph shows how the size of a population of **deer** and a population of **wolves** living in the same area changed over time.

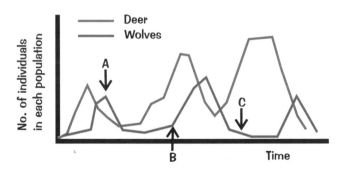

a)   Describe the pattern in the changing sizes of these two populations.

....

....

b)   Explain why the two populations are connected in this way.

....

c)   At one point during the period covered by this graph, the wolves were affected by a disease. Underline one of the options below to show when this was.

   At point A   **At point B**   **At point C**

d)   What effect did the disease have on the size of the **deer** population? Suggest why this happened.

....

....

Variation in Plants and Animals

Q1   Complete this passage by circling the **best** word or phrase from each highlighted pair.

> Usually, organisms of the same species **have differences** / **are identical**.
>
> This is partly because different organisms have different **genes** / **cells**, which
>
> they inherit from their parents. **Siblings** / **Identical twins** are exceptions to this.
>
> But even these usually have some different features, such as **hair style** / **eye colour**,
>
> and that is due to their **diet** / **environment**. The differences between individual
>
> organisms are known as **variation** / **inheritance**.

Q2   Helen and Stephanie are identical twins. Helen has dark hair and Stephanie is blonde.

    a)   Do you think that these are Helen and Stephanie's natural hair colours? Explain your answer.

        ....

        ....

    b)   Helen weighs 7 kg more than Stephanie. Say whether this is due to genes, environment or both, and explain your answer.

        ....

        ....

    c)   Stephanie has a birthmark on her shoulder shaped like Wayne Rooney. Helen doesn't. Do you think birthmarks are caused by your genes? Explain why.

        ....

        ....

Q3   Mr O'Riley breeds racehorses. He breeds his best black racing stallion, Snowball, with his best black racing mare, Goldie.

    a)   Why is there no guarantee that any foal born will be a champion racer?

        ....

        ....

    b)   Will the colour of the newborn foal be due to genes or to environment?

        ....

Variation in Plants and Animals

Q4 The peppered moth is an insect that is often found on tree bark and is preyed on by birds. There are two varieties of peppered moth — a light form and a dark form. Until the 1850s, the light form was more common, but after then the dark form increased a lot, particularly near cities.

Moths on tree bark in unpolluted area

Moths on tree bark in polluted area

a) Why do you think the lighter variety of the peppered moth was more common originally?

....

....

Hint: Use the diagrams to help you.

b) In the 1850s, the Industrial Revolution began — there was rapid growth in heavy industries in Britain. Why do you think the number of dark moths increased after this time?

....

....

c) Do you think a difference in genes or in environment would cause a dark moth to suddenly appear in a population of light moths? ....

Q5 Nazneen grows three strawberry plants and three sunflowers.

a) Why do the strawberry plants look so different to the sunflower plants?

....

b) Sunflower plants reproduce by sexual reproduction. Why could Nazneen not expect her three sunflower plants to be exactly the same height?

....

....

c) Nazneen's strawberry plants were grown by asexual reproduction. However, her three strawberry plants are not all exactly the same height. Explain why this might be.

....

....

Genes, Chromosomes and DNA

Q1   Complete the passage using some of the words given below.

DNA	nucleus	genes	chromosomes	membrane	allele

Each cell of the body contains a structure called the ....

This structure contains strands of genetic information, packaged into ....

These strands are made of a chemical called ....

Sections of genetic material that control different characteristics are called ....

Q2   Write out these structures in order of size, **starting with the smallest**.

nucleus	gene	chromosome	cell

1. ....   2. ....   3. ....   4. ....

Q3   Which of the following is the correct definition of the term **'alleles'**? Underline your choice.

'Alleles' is the collective term for all the genes found on a pair of chromosomes.

'Alleles' are different forms of the same gene.

'Alleles' are identical organisms produced by asexual reproduction.

Q4   Only one of the following statements is true. Tick the correct one.

There are two chromosome 7s in a human nucleus, both from the person's mother. ☐

There are two chromosome 7s in a human nucleus, both from the person's father. ☐

There are two chromosome 7s in a human nucleus, one from each parent. ☐

There is only one chromosome 7 in a human nucleus. ☐

Q5   The human chromosome 15 contains a gene that is involved in controlling eye colour. How many chromosome 15s would you expect to find in each of the following cells?

a)   A cell in the retina of the eye.   ....

b)   A muscle cell.   ....

c)   A sperm cell.   ....

Top Tips:
First of all you need to know exactly what's meant by genes, alleles, DNA, chromosomes, etc. And don't forget that virtually all organisms have two of each chromosome in their body cells.

Reproduction

Q1   Circle the correct words in each statement below to complete the sentences.

a)   Sexual reproduction involves **one** / **two** individual(s).

b)   The cells that are involved in asexual reproduction are called **parent cells** / **gametes**.

c)   Asexual reproduction produces offspring with **identical** / **different** genes to the parent.

d)   In sexual reproduction the sperm cell contains **the same number of** / **half as many** chromosomes as the **fertilised** egg.

e)   **Asexual** / **Sexual** reproduction creates offspring with different characteristics to the parent(s).

Q2   Complete the following sentences.

a)   Offspring that are identical to their parent are called ....

b)   The male gamete is a ....

c)   The process that occurs when two gametes fuse is ....

Q3   Lucy cut her hand, but a week later she noticed that the cut had almost disappeared. The skin covering it looked just the same as the skin on the rest of her hand. This happened by the same process as **asexual reproduction**.

a)   Where did the new skin cells on Lucy's hand come from?

....

....

b)   Suggest why the skin on Lucy's hand looked the same as it had before she had cut herself.

....

....

c)   Suggest why it took a week for the cut to heal.

....

....

Q4   Explain how a human baby receives genes from both its father and its mother, but still only has 46 chromosomes in its cells.

....

....

....

Cloning

Q1 Joe has a herd of cows and he wants them all to have calves, but he **only** wants to breed from his champion bull and prize cow.

a) Name a method Joe could use to achieve this. ....

b) Describe the steps involved in this method in detail.

....

....

....

c) Which of the animals involved in this process will be genetically identical?

....

d) Give one disadvantage of this method.

....

....

Q2 a) Describe the process that was used to create **Dolly the sheep**.

....

....

....

b) Explain how this process could be adapted and used to help treat problems such as kidney disease.

....

....

Q3 a) Name the **two** methods commonly used by man to produce clones of plants.

....

b) Give **two** advantages and **one** disadvantage of cloning plants using methods like these.

Advantage 1: ....

Advantage 2: ....

Disadvantage: ....

Q4 Discuss the **ethical** issues involved in using **embryonic stem cells** to treat diseases.

....

....

....

Genetic Engineering

Q1 Billy has **cystic fibrosis**. Say briefly how genetic engineering could be used to help him.

....

....

Q2 Some people are **worried** about genetic engineering.

a) Explain why some people are concerned about genetic engineering.

....

....

b) Do you think that scientists should be carrying out genetic engineering? Explain your answer.

....

....

....

Q3 Fill in the gaps in the passage below to explain **how** genetic engineering is carried out.

The useful .... is 'cut' from the donor organism's chromosome using

.... The same .... are then used to cut the host

organism's chromosome and the useful .... is inserted. This technique is

known as gene ....

Q4 Explain how genetic engineering can be used to produce large amounts of human insulin in a short time.

....

....

Q5 Look carefully at this headline about a new type of **GM salmon**.

> **Monster food? Scientists insert a growth hormone gene and create fish that grow much faster than ever before!**

Some scientists have warned that the GM salmon should be tightly controlled so they don't escape into the sea. What might happen if the GM salmon were allowed to escape?

....

....

Genetic Engineering

Q6   Read the article below about **GM crops** and answer the questions that follow.

There are many reasons for genetically modifying crops. Two important reasons are to make them pest-resistant and to make them resistant to herbicides (weedkillers).

At the moment no one's growing any GM crops in the UK. Recently, though, some farmers took part in crop trials set up by the Government, to see what effects growing herbicide-tolerant GM crops might have on wildlife. There were four kinds of crops in the trials — beet, spring oilseed rape, maize and winter oilseed rape.

Fields of various sizes were chosen for the study. In each case, the farmer split one of their normal fields in half. They then grew a 'normal' crop in one half and its GM equivalent in the other. Apart from that, they did everything normally — ploughing the field, adding fertiliser etc. in the same way as they usually would. The only difference was with herbicides — with the GM crops, the farmers followed instructions about how much of which herbicides to use, and when to apply them. They applied herbicides to the 'normal' crop as they usually would.

As the crops grew, the government researchers counted the number of weeds growing, and the number of weed seeds produced in each half of the field. They also monitored the populations of insects, slugs, spiders and other wildlife.

The researchers found that with three crops (beet, spring oilseed rape and winter oilseed rape), growing normal crops was better for wildlife — they found more butterflies and bees on the normal crops. They also found more flowering weeds (the kinds that butterflies and bees prefer) on the side with the normal crops. With maize, oddly, the opposite seemed to be true — there were more weeds, and more butterflies and bees, around the GM crops.

a)   Explain the **purpose** of the trial described in the article.

....

....

b)   i)   Suggest why each field was divided in half rather than choosing separate fields for normal and GM crops.

....

....

Farmer Gideon had a brand new combine harvester and he wasn't going to give anyone the keys.

ii)   Give two things that were done in the same way by the farmers for the GM crops and for the normal crops. Suggest why these things were kept constant.

....

....

iii)   Give one thing that was done differently for the GM crops and for the normal crops. Suggest why this was not kept constant for both types of crop.

....

....

Genetic Engineering

c) Herbicides were used on **both** the normal and the GM crops in this trial.

    i) Explain why fewer weeds normally grow among herbicide-resistant crops.

....

....

    ii) Explain how growing herbicide-resistant crops in the UK could benefit:

farmers. ....

....

shoppers buying these products. ....

....

d) The result for the **maize** crop was surprising. Tick the box next to the **correct** statement below.

☐ The result was surprising because wildlife preferred the GM maize even though there were fewer weeds.

☐ The result was surprising because there were more weeds with the GM crop even though more herbicide was used.

☐ The result was surprising because bees and butterflies are usually repelled by GM crops.

e) Some people are **worried** that growing GM crops will lead to a reduction in **biodiversity**.

    i) Do you think that the results of this trial support the above fear? Explain your answer.

....

....

    ii) Give two other reasons why people are concerned about GM crops.

....

....

    iii) Suggest one possible reason for the unusual result seen with the maize crop in this trial.

....

....

Evolution

Q1 a) Roughly how many species have so far been identified on Earth?
Circle the correct number from the options listed below.

1500   15 000   150 000   1 500 000

b) There are actually many more species than this. Some scientists think there might be as many as 100 million species on Earth. Suggest why this figure is so much bigger than the figure in part a).

....

....

Q2 Dinosaurs, mammoths and dodos are all animals that are now **extinct.**

a) What does the term 'extinct' mean?

....

....

b) How do we know about extinct animals?

....

....

Q3 Fossils of shells were found in a sample of rock.

Think about what replaces the tissues of organisms as they slowly decay.

a) Explain how fossils form.

....

....

....

b) Why are fossils of animals more common than those of plants?

....

c) Fossils were found in this sample of rock.
Explain why scientists think that fossil B is older.

Fossil A

Fossil B

....

....

Top Tips: My biology teacher was a bit of an old fossil... expert. Some people think fossils are really boring (picture the reaction when Ross from Friends starts going on about them) but the fossil record has provided evidence of all kinds of weird and wonderful creatures that are now long gone. Think Tyrannosaurus rex and gigantic guinea pigs — wow.

Evolution

Q4 A and B are fossilised bones from the legs of ancestors of the modern horse. Some scientists believe that animals with legs like fossil A gradually developed into animals with legs like fossil B.

a) Suggest **two** reasons why this change may have happened.

....

....

....

....

A

B

b) It is thought that there was a stage in the development of the horse between A and B, during which the leg bone would have looked like C. Suggest why no fossils of C have been found.

C

....

....

Q5 One idea of **how life began** is that simple organic molecules were brought to Earth by **comets**. It's not known if this is right.

a) What do we call this type of scientific idea? ....

b) Suggest why this idea has neither been generally accepted or completely rejected by all scientists.

....

c) Give another scientific idea for how life began.

....

....

Q6 Some animals were exposed to a chemical which damaged the **DNA** in their **skin cells**. These animals developed skin cancer. They then had offspring, **none** of which developed skin cancer.

a) What do we call a change in DNA?

....

b) Why was the skin cancer not passed on to the offspring?

....

....

c) Some of the offspring had new mutations in the DNA in each of their cells. These had not been present in all the cells of their parents and were thought to be due to the chemical. Which cells in the bodies of the parent animals do you think had been damaged, other than the skin cells?

....

Evolution

Q7 Giraffes used to have much **shorter** necks than they do today.

   a) The statements below explain Darwin's theory about how their neck length changed.
   Write numbers in the boxes to show the **order** the statements should be in.

   ☐ The giraffes competed for food from low branches. This food started
   to become scarce. Many giraffes died before they could breed.

   ☐ More long-necked giraffes survived to breed, so more giraffes were born with long necks.

   ☐ A giraffe was born with a longer neck than normal.
   The long-necked giraffe was able to eat more food.

   ☐ All giraffes had short necks.

   ☐ The long-necked giraffe survived to have lots of
   offspring that all had longer necks.

   ☐ All giraffes had long necks.

   b) Lamarck's theory of how giraffes evolved to have long necks was different from Darwin's.
   How would Lamarck have explained their evolution?

   ....

   ....

Q8 **Sickle cell anaemia** is a serious **genetic** disease that makes it harder for a person
   to carry enough oxygen in their blood. In Europe the disease is very **rare**.
   However, in Africa sickle cell anaemia is more **common**.

   a) Explain why natural selection may act against people with sickle cell anaemia in Europe.

   ....

   ....

   b) Malaria is also more common in Africa. People who carry a gene for sickle cell anaemia are more
   resistant to malaria. Explain how natural selection means there's more sickle cell anaemia in Africa.

   ....

   ....

Q9 A student incubated a sample of bacteria on an agar plate. The bacteria multiplied to form a
   plaque. He then added an **antibiotic** to the bacteria. Most of the bacteria died. He incubated
   the plate again and the remaining bacteria reproduced to form a new plaque. He added the
   same antibiotic to the bacterial plaque and **nothing happened**. Explain these results.

   ....

   ....

Human Impact on the Environment

Q1   Circle the correct word to complete each sentence below.

a)   The size of the human population now is **bigger** / **smaller** than it was 1000 years ago.

b)   The growth of the human population now is **slower** / **faster** than it was 1000 years ago.

c)   The human impact on the environment now is **less** / **greater** than it was 1000 years ago.

Q2   The graph below shows the amount of sulfur dioxide released in the UK between 1970 and 2003.

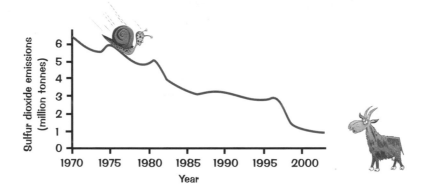

a)   In which year shown on the graph were sulfur dioxide emissions highest?   ....

b)   Approximately how much sulfur dioxide was emitted in 2003?   ....

c)   Name one problem caused by sulfur dioxide.

      ....

Q3   One way to assess a person's impact on the Earth is to use an **ecological footprint**. This involves calculating **how many Earths** would be needed if everyone lived like that person. It takes into account things like the amount of **waste** the person produces and how much **energy** they use.

a)   Two men calculate their ecological footprints. Eight Earths would be needed to support everyone in the way John lives. Half an Earth would be enough to support everyone in the way Derek lives.

      i) One of the men lives in a UK city, and one in rural Kenya. Who is more likely to live where?

          ....

      ii) Tick any of the following that are possible reasons for the difference in results.

          ☐ John buys more belongings, which use more raw materials to manufacture.

          ☐ John has central heating in his home but Derek has a wood fire.

          ☐ John throws away less waste.

          ☐ John drives a car and Derek rides a bicycle.

b)   Suggest one thing John could do to reduce the size of his ecological footprint.

      ....

Human Impact on the Environment

Q4   The size of the Earth's population has an impact on our environment.

a) Use the table below to plot a graph on the grid, showing how the world's human population has changed over the last 1000 years.

NO. OF PEOPLE (BILLIONS)	YEAR
0.3	1000
0.4	1200
0.4	1400
0.6	1600
1.0	1800
1.7	1900
6.1	2000

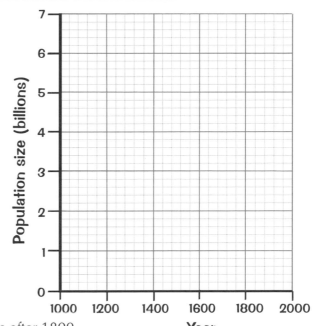

b) Suggest two reasons for the sudden increase after 1800.

....

....

Q5   As the human population **grows** we need more **food**. Modern farming methods can increase the amount of food grown, but they may harm the environment.

a) Give three types of chemicals used in modern farming.

1. ....

2. ....

3. ....

b) Explain how chemicals such as these may affect the environment.

....

....

....

Top Tips:

There's lots to think about with this topic. It's the kind of thing you might get a longer answer question on in an exam, where you have to weigh up all the different arguments. And of course, examiners can't get enough of that graph where the human population suddenly goes shooting up — they love it.

The Greenhouse Effect

Q1   Underline the statements below about the greenhouse effect that are **true**.

The greenhouse effect is needed for life on Earth as we know it.

Greenhouse gases include carbon dioxide and sulfur dioxide.

The greenhouse effect causes acid rain.

Increasing amounts of greenhouse gases may lead to global warming.

Q2   The Earth receives energy from the **Sun**. It radiates much of this energy back towards space.

a)   Explain the role of the greenhouse gases in keeping the Earth warm.

....

....

b)   What would happen if there were no greenhouse gases?

....

c)   In recent years the amounts of greenhouse gases in the atmosphere have increased.
Explain how this leads to global warming.

....

....

Q3   **Deforestation** increases the amount of **carbon dioxide** released
into the atmosphere and decreases the amount removed.

a)   Explain how this happens.

....

....

....

....

b)   Give three reasons why humans cut forests down.

....

....

c)   Give two other examples of human activities that release carbon dioxide into the atmosphere.

....

The Greenhouse Effect

Q4   The graph below shows changes in **global temperature** since 1859.

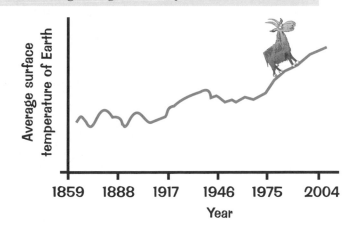

a)   Describe the trend shown on the graph.

....

b)   The next graph shows how current levels of three gases compare to their levels before the Industrial Revolution.

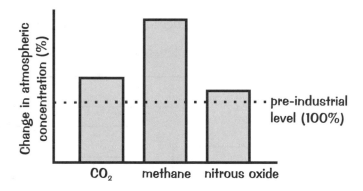

i)   Which gas has had the biggest percentage increase in concentration? ....

ii)   Give one source of this gas.

....

c)   What conclusion can you draw from these two graphs?
Did one of the changes definitely cause the other?

....

....

....

Top Tips:

Climate change isn't a subject that scientists know all about. Ideas about what's happening and the possible long-term effects are evolving all the time, and it's hard to find two scientists that totally agree with one another. You've just got to be aware that there are different theories.

48

Climate Change

Q1   One UK newspaper said that global warming will be good for the UK because people will be able to have more barbecues. Do you think they're right? Explain your answer.

....

....

Q2   Two university students carried out **observations**. Student A noticed that a glacier was melting. Student B noticed that daffodils were flowering earlier in 2006 than in 2005. Both students concluded that this was due to **global warming**. Are they right? Explain your answer.

....

....

Q3   These statements help explain how **global warming** may lead to floods and temperature decreases. Use them to complete the **flow chart**, which has one box filled in to start you off.

Low-lying areas are at risk of flooding.   Some areas (maybe the UK) get colder.

Ocean currents are disrupted.   Higher temperatures make ice melt.

Cold fresh water enters the ocean.   Sea levels start to rise.

| The seas get warmer and expand. |
| 1 |
| 3 |
| 2 |
| 5 |
| 4 |
| 6 |

Q4   Scientists are collecting **evidence** to try to support or disprove the **theory** of global warming.

   a)   What is meant by evidence and theory?

   evidence: ....

   theory: ....

   b)   Give examples of the sort of data that scientists are collecting about climate change.

....

....

Sustainable Development

Q1 Humans can affect the **environment** in lots of ways.

a) Give two ways that humans can have a negative effect on the environment.

....

b) Explain why some of the negative effects caused by humans cannot easily be reversed.

....

....

Q2 **Ecosystems** like rainforests contain many different **species**. If we destroy rainforests we risk making species extinct and **reducing biodiversity**.

a) Define the term '**ecosystem**'. ....

....

b) What is meant by '**reducing biodiversity**'?

....

c) What are the implications for humans of reducing biodiversity?

....

....

....

Q3 Mayfly larvae and sludge worms are often studied to see how much **sewage** is in water.

a) What is the name for an organism used in this way? ....

Juanita recorded the number of each species in water samples taken at three different distances away from a sewage outlet. Her results are shown on the right.

Distance (km)	No. of mayfly larvae	No. of sludge worms
1	3	20
2	11	14
3	23	7

b) Give one thing that she would have to do to make this experiment a fair test.

....

c) What can you conclude about the two organisms from these results?

....

....

d) Suggest why sewage may decrease the number of mayfly larvae.

....

....

Mixed Questions — Biology 1b

Q1   The graph shows how the **body temperatures** of a camel and a goat change throughout the day in a hot desert.

body temperature

camel

goat

6 am   12 noon   6 pm   12 midnight

a)   Between 6 am and 12 noon, what happened to the body temperature:

   i) of the camel? ....

   ii) of the goat? ....

b)   Which one of the animals keeps cool by sweating? ....

c)   Explain why animals that use sweating to keep cool can't survive well in deserts.

   ....

d)   Camels were a traditional means of transport in the desert. However, more people are now using 4-wheel-drive jeeps. Explain why a camel is a **more sustainable** form of transport than a jeep.

   ....

   ....

Q2   An experiment was done with two **fertilised natterjack toad eggs**. The eggs came from completely different parents. The nucleus of **egg A** was put into **egg B**, and the nucleus of egg B was **removed** (see the diagram on the right).

A   B

Nucleus from A
is inserted into B

Nucleus from B
is discarded

a)   Egg **B** grew into a toad. Would you expect it to look more like the parents of egg **A** or the parents of egg **B**? Explain your answer.

   ....

b)   The technique used to create Dolly the sheep also involved removing genetic material from an egg cell. However, Dolly was a **clone**, whereas the toad produced in this experiment was not. Explain why this is.

   ....

   ....

c)   There are now far fewer natterjack toads than there were a century ago. This is largely due to **human impact**. Suggest **two** ways that humans may have caused their numbers to decline.

   ....

   ....

d)   **Competition** with other amphibians has also had an effect on the number of natterjack toads. Suggest **two** things that the toads may have been competing for.

   ....

e)   Because of their permeable skin, amphibians are '**sensitive indicator species**'. Explain what this term means. ....

   ....

Mixed Questions — Biology 1b

Q3 The table shows four people, identified by the letters **M**, **Q**, **X** and **Z**.

Characteristic	Code-name			
	M	Q	X	Z
They have a suntan	✓	✓		
They are male	✓	✓	✓	
They can roll their tongue	✓		✓	
Natural hair colour is brown	✓	✓	✓	✓
They have bleached blond hair			✓	✓
They have brown eyes	✓	✓	✓	

a) Use the information in the table to identify which two people could be identical twins.

....

b) Explain your answer.

....

....

Q4 The normal numbers of **chromosomes** in the body cells of some different species are:

> donkeys — 31 pairs of chromosomes   horses — 32 pairs of chromosomes
>
> lions — 19 pairs of chromosomes   tigers — 19 pairs of chromosomes

Mating between different, closely-related species occasionally results in offspring. However, the offspring are usually **sterile**. For example, a **mule** is a cross between a donkey and a horse, and a **liger** is a cross between a lion and a tiger.

a) Use the information above to work out the number of chromosomes in the body cells of a mule.

Hint: Think about the number of chromosomes in the gametes of donkeys and horses.

....

b) Mules are almost always sterile, but ligers can occasionally produce offspring of their own. Explain this by considering the number of chromosomes of ligers and mules.

....

....

Q5 Scientists tried to **genetically modify** some bacteria. They inserted a piece of DNA containing both the human gene for **growth hormone** and a gene for **penicillin resistance** into a bacterium. Afterwards, the bacteria were grown on agar plates containing penicillin.

a) Why were the bacteria grown on plates containing penicillin?

Hint: It's hard to tell by looking if the growth hormone gene has been inserted correctly.

....

....

b) Give **two advantages** of producing growth hormone with bacteria, rather than by other methods.

....

....

c) The bacteria produced were all genetically identical. What type of reproduction do you think took place?

....

Biology 1b — Evolution and Environment

Mixed Questions — Biology 1b

Q6 In the Galapagos Islands, different varieties of **giant tortoise** are found on different islands. For example, where the main available food is grass, the tortoises have a dome-shaped shell. However, where the main food is tall cacti, the tortoises have a saddle-backed shell, which allows them to raise their heads higher to feed.

dome-shelled tortoise   saddle-back tortoise

a) Charles Darwin was particularly interested in animals like the tortoise on the Galapagos Islands. Explain the significance of these animals for Darwin.

....

....

b) Why do islands often have their own species of animals?

....

....

c) Explain the difference between **evolution** and **natural selection**.

....

....

d) The Galapagos Islands have been described as an '**oasis for biodiversity**'. Explain what this means.

....

e) **Galapagos penguins** are the rarest **penguins** in the world. Their numbers have fallen in recent years and scientists believe that this is partly due to **changing ocean currents**, which have affected the penguins' food sources. Explain how **humans** are contributing to this problem.

....

....

f) The Galapagos Islands are becoming an increasingly popular tourist destination, but visitors to the islands can damage the fragile ecosystems. There are calls for tourism in the Galapagos Islands to be '**sustainably developed**'. Explain what is meant by this phrase.

....

....

g) There is a rule which forbids tourists from bringing '**any live material**' to the Galapagos Islands. Suggest why this is.

....

....

Atoms and Elements

Q1 a)   Draw a diagram of a **helium atom**.

b)   Label each type of **particle** on your diagram.

Helium has 2 of each type of particle.

Q2   Look at these diagrams of substances. Circle the ones that contain only **one element**.

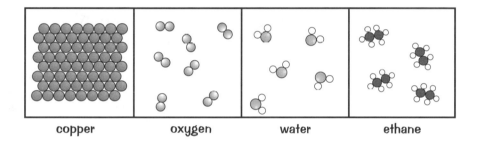

copper   oxygen   water   ethane

Q3   Many everyday substances, such as gold and aluminium, are **elements**. Other substances such as water and sugar are not.

Explain what this means in terms of the **atoms** in them.

....

....

Q4   Fill in the blanks to complete these sentences.

a)   The number of .... in an atom tells us which type of element it is.

b)   The nucleus of an atom consists of .... and ....

c)   Electrons are found in .... around the ....

d)   Hydrogen has the smallest atoms. A hydrogen atom contains only one .... and

one ....

The Periodic Table

Q1 Choose from these words to fill in the blanks.

left-hand   right-hand   horizontal   similar   different
vertical   metals   non-metals   transition

a)   A group in the periodic table is a .... line of elements.

b)   Most of the elements in the periodic table are ....

c)   The elements between group II and group III are called .... metals.

d)   Non-metals are on the .... side of the periodic table.

e)   Elements in the same group have .... properties.

Q2 Argon is an extremely **unreactive** gas. Use the periodic table to give the names of two more gases that you would expect to have similar properties to argon.

1. ....

2. ....

Q3 Use the **periodic table** to complete the following table.

Element	Symbol	Reaction with magnesium	Formula of substance formed
Fluorine			MgF_2
	Cl	burns quickly	$MgCl_2$
Bromine			

Q4 Mendeleev (who **drew up** the periodic table) left gaps where he predicted undiscovered elements would fit. One of the gaps he left was **below silicon**. How did the **arrangement** of the periodic table help scientists know when they had found the missing element?

....

....

....

Compounds and Mixtures

Q1   **Seawater** is a **mixture** of water and various dissolved substances, such as sodium chloride (table salt). **Water** is a **compound** of **hydrogen** and **oxygen**.

Are these statements true or false?   **True   False**

a)   The substances in seawater are not chemically bonded to each other.   ☐   ☐

b)   Water can be separated into hydrogen and oxygen by boiling it.   ☐   ☐

c)   When seawater is heated until all the water evaporates, the only thing that is left behind is table salt.   ☐   ☐

d)   The formula for water is H_2O because it contains two hydrogen atoms joined to one oxygen atom.   ☐   ☐

Q2   Choose from these words to fill in the blanks. Some words may be used more than once.

compounds   different   bonds   identical   separate
electrons   elements   taking

When atoms of different elements react they form bonds by giving away, taking or sharing

.... The chemicals produced are called .... and are

usually very difficult to .... using physical methods. The properties of

compounds are .... from those of the elements used to make them.

Mixtures are usually easier to .... because there are no chemical

.... between their different parts.

Q3   Crude oil contains a lot of different substances. Most of them contain carbon joined to hydrogen and are called **hydrocarbons** (e.g. octane, C_8H_{18}, and pentane, C_5H_{12}). The majority of these hydrocarbons are **liquids**. To separate them the oil is **distilled**. Explain why **distillation** is a good way to **separate** these liquids.

....

....

Top Tips: Compounds always contain two or more different elements **bonded together**. Mixtures also contain two or more elements and the particles in them can be compounds. The difference is that mixtures contain at least two sorts of particles that are **not chemically joined** together.

Chemistry 1a — Products from Rocks

<u>Compounds and Mixtures</u>

Q4 Andy puts some **magnesium metal** powder (which is a silver coloured powder) into a container of **oxygen** gas. Andy **heats** the contents of the container, allows them to cool and then describes what he can see in the container. Here are his results:

Appearance of powder	
Before heating	After heating
Silver coloured powder	White powder

a) Are magnesium and oxygen **elements**, **compounds** or **mixtures**?

....

b) At the end of the experiment is the powder a **mixture** or a **compound**?

....

c) What happens in the container to make the appearance of the contents change?

....

d) Write a **word equation** for the reaction that takes place in the container.

....

e) Would it be easier for Andy to use **physical methods** to separate the contents of the container **before** or **after** he heats them?

....

Q5 Circle the formula that contains the **most nitrogen** atoms.

NH_4Cl $(NH_4)_2CO_3$ N_2O_5 NO_2

$Al(NO_3)_3$ NH_3 NH_3NO_3

> ## <u>Top Tips:</u> Sometimes you'll see formulas for chemicals that you've never heard of. Don't get stressed out — the same rules for identifying the elements that are in them apply to them all. So once you've got the hang of some simple ones like H_2O, you'll be able to do them all night long.

Balancing Equations

Q1 Which of the following equations are **balanced** correctly?

	Correctly balanced	Incorrectly balanced

a) $H_2 + Cl_2 \rightarrow 2HCl$ ☐ ☐

b) $CuO + HCl \rightarrow CuCl_2 + H_2O$ ☐ ☐

c) $N_2 + H_2 \rightarrow NH_3$ ☐ ☐

d) $CuO + H_2 \rightarrow Cu + H_2O$ ☐ ☐

e) $CaCO_3 \rightarrow CaO + CO_2$ ☐ ☐

Q2 Here is the equation for the formation of carbon monoxide in a poorly ventilated gas fire. It is **not** balanced correctly.

$$C + O_2 \rightarrow CO$$

Circle the **correctly balanced** version of this equation.

$$C + O_2 \rightarrow CO_2$$
$$C + O_2 \rightarrow 2CO$$
$$2C + O_2 \rightarrow 2CO$$

Q3 In a book, this is the description of a reaction: "**methane** (CH_4) can be burnt in **oxygen** (O_2) to make **carbon dioxide** (CO_2) and **water** (H_2O)".

a) What are the **reactants** and the **products** in this reaction?

Reactants: .... Products: ....

b) Write the **word equation** for this reaction.

....

c) Write the **balanced symbol equation** for the reaction.

....

Don't forget the oxygen ends up in both products

> **Top Tips:** The most important thing to remember with balancing equations is that you can't change the **little numbers** — if you do that then you'll change the substance into something completely different. Just take your time and work through everything logically.

58

<u>*Balancing Equations*</u>

Q4   Write out the balanced **symbol** equations for the unbalanced picture equations below.

a)   Na Na   +   Cl Cl   →   Na Cl / Na Cl

....

> You can draw more pictures to help you balance the unbalanced ones.

b)   Li   +   O O   →   Li O Li

....

c)   Mg O C O O   +   H Cl   →   Cl Mg Cl   +   H O H   +   O C O

....

d)   Li   +   H O H / H O H   →   Li O H   +   H H

....

Q5   Add **one** number to each of these equations so that they are **correctly balanced**.

a) $CuO + HBr \rightarrow CuBr_2 + H_2O$

b) $H_2 + Br_2 \rightarrow HBr$

> You need to have 2 bromines and 2 hydrogens on the left-hand side.

c) $Mg + O_2 \rightarrow 2MgO$

d) $2NaOH + H_2SO_4 \rightarrow Na_2SO_4 + H_2O$

Q6   **Balance** these equations by adding in numbers.

a) $NaOH + AlBr_3 \rightarrow NaBr + Al(OH)_3$

b) $FeCl_2 + Cl_2 \rightarrow FeCl_3$

c) $N_2 + H_2 \rightarrow NH_3$

d) $Fe + O_2 \rightarrow Fe_2O_3$

$Fe_2O_3 + 3CO \rightarrow 2Fe + 3CO_2$

e) $NH_3 + O_2 \rightarrow NO + H_2O$

Chemistry 1a — Products from Rocks

Using Limestone

Q1 a) What is the **chemical name** for limestone?

....

b) What is the **chemical name** for quicklime?

....

Q2 Use the words below to fill the gaps in the passage.

sand	sodium carbonate	wood	concrete	clay	limestone

Heating powdered .... with clay in a kiln makes cement.

When cement is mixed with water, gravel and sand it makes ....,

which is a very common building material.   Heating limestone with

.... and .... makes glass.

Q3 **Carbonates** decompose to form two products.

a) Name the **two** products formed when limestone is heated.

1. ....

2. ....

b) What **solid** would you expect to be formed when **magnesium carbonate** is heated?

....

c) Write a **symbol equation** for the reaction that occurs when **copper carbonate** ($CuCO_3$) is heated.

....

Q4 The hills of Northern England are dotted with the remains of **lime kilns** where **limestone** ($CaCO_3$) was heated by farmers to make **quicklime** (CaO).

a) Write a word equation for the reaction that takes place in a lime kiln.

....

b) Quicklime reacts violently with water to make **slaked lime**, calcium hydroxide ($Ca(OH)_2$). Slaked lime is a weak alkali.

What do farmers use slaked lime for?

....

Using Limestone

Q5   Heating metal carbonates is an example of **thermal decomposition**.

a)   Explain what **thermal decomposition** means.

....

b)   **Calcium oxide** and **calcium carbonate** are both white solids.
How could you tell the difference between them?

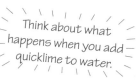

Think about what happens when you add quicklime to water.

....

c)   How could you prove that carbon dioxide is produced when a metal carbonate is heated?

....

Q6   This passage is about **limestone extraction** in the Peak District National Park.
Read the extract and then answer the questions that follow.

The Peak District National Park covers about 1500 km^2 of land. Tourism is very important — a lot of people visit the area to enjoy the countryside. Limestone quarrying is also part of the local economy and there are 12 large quarries in the park. Some people aren't keen on all this — they say that quarrying is spoiling the natural beauty of the landscape, and discouraging tourists from visiting.

The Peak District

The limestone in the Peak District is very pure. It has been used locally in agriculture, and burned in lime kilns, for many years. When canals and railways were built in the area, limestone quarried in the park could be taken further afield, for use in industries elsewhere.
This continues today, and is another cause for concern — large lorries clog up narrow roads and disturb the peace and quiet in small villages.

A lot of limestone has been dug out of the Peak District. In 1990, 8.5 million tonnes of limestone were quarried from the Peak District National Park — more than five times as much as in 1951. This limestone is used in several different industries (the figures below are for 1989).

Use	Percentage
Aggregate (for road-building etc.)	55.8%
Cement	23%
Chemicals	17%
Iron and steel	4%
Agriculture	0.2%

Using Limestone

a) What makes the **limestone** in the Peak District particularly useful?

....

b) Approximately how many tonnes of limestone were quarried in 1951?

....

c) Describe one way in which limestone has been used locally in the Peak District.

....

d) State **three problems** that are caused by quarrying limestone in the Peak District.

1. ....

2. ....

3. ....

e) **i)** How was limestone originally **transported away** from the Peak District?

....

ii) How is limestone **transported** today?

....

f) Do you think that the person who wrote the article is in favour of quarrying or against it? Explain the reasons for your answer.

....

....

g) Complete this table showing the amount of limestone quarried from the Peak District in 1989.

Use	Percentage	Total amount quarried in tonnes
Aggregate (for road-building etc.)	55.8%	
Cement	23%	
Chemicals	17%	
Iron and steel	4%	
Agriculture	0.2%	

Using Limestone

Q7 Many of the products used to build houses are made with limestone.
Circle the materials that have **no** connection to limestone.

glass

paint

bricks

cement

granite

concrete

Q8 In Norway **powdered limestone** is added to lakes that have been damaged by acid rain.

a) Name the process that takes place when the powdered limestone reacts with the acid in the lake.

....

b) Explain why powdered limestone is also used in the chimneys at power stations.

....

....

Q9 Limestone is a useful rock but **quarrying** it causes some **problems**.

a) Describe two problems that quarrying limestone can cause.

1. ....

2. ....

b) Explain how limestone quarries may benefit the local community.

....

....

Q10 What are the **advantages** of using **concrete** instead of these traditional building materials?

a) Wood: ....

b) Metals: ....

c) Bricks: ....

Properties of Metals

Q1 Most **metals** that are used to make everyday objects are found in the **central section** of the periodic table.

a) What name is given to this group of metals?

....

b) Why could metals from this group be used to make electrical wires?

....

Q2 This table shows some of the **properties** of four different **metals**.

Metal	Heat conduction	Cost	Resistance to corrosion	Strength
1	average	high	excellent	good
2	average	medium	good	excellent
3	excellent	low	good	good
4	low	high	average	poor

Use the information in the table to choose which metal would be **best** for making each of the following:

a) Saucepan bases ....

b) Car bodies ....

c) A statue to be placed in a town centre ....

Think about how long a statue would have to last for.

Q3 What **properties** would you look for if you were asked to choose a **metal** suitable for making knives and forks?

....

....

....

Top Tips: Remember most elements are metals and most metals have similar properties. But don't be a fool and think they're all identical — there are lots of little differences which make them useful for different things. Some metals are pretty weird, for example mercury is liquid at room temperature, which means it's not ideal for making cars.

Properties of Metals

Q4   In an experiment some identically sized rods of different materials (A, B, C and D) were **heated** at one end and **temperature sensors** were connected to the other ends. The results are shown in the graph.

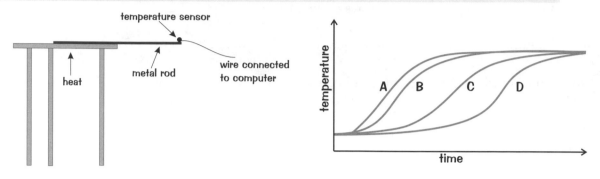

a)   Which two rods do you think were made from metals?

....

b)   Which of the metals was the best conductor of heat and how can you tell?

....

Q5   All metals have a similar structure. This explains why many of them have similar properties.

a)   Draw a labelled diagram of a typical metal structure.

Think about the reasons why metals are good conductors.

b)   What is unusual about the electrons in a metal?

....

Q6   Imagine that a space probe has brought a sample of a new element back from Mars. Scientists think that the element is a **metal**, but they aren't certain. Give **three properties** they could look for to provide evidence that the element is a **metal**.

1. ....

2. ....

3. ....

Top Tips: Ever wondered why we don't make bridges out of platinum? Cost is a big factor in the use of metals, so even if a metal is perfect for a job it might not be used because it's too expensive. The cheapest metals are the ones that are both common and easy to extract from their ores.

Metals from Rocks

Q1   **Copper** is used to make electrical wires.

a)   Copper can be extracted from its ore by reduction with carbon.
Why **can't** copper produced in this way be used for electrical wires?

....

b)   How is copper that **is** suitable for making electrical wires produced?

....

c)   Give another **common use** of copper.

....

Q2   Copper objects such as old pipes can be **recycled**.
Give **two** reasons why it is important to recycle copper.

1. ....

2. ....

Q3   The following extract is taken from a press release from a scientific research company.
Read the extract and then answer the questions below.

Here at Copperextra we are very excited about our latest developments.

Within six months we expect to be extracting pure copper from material that would usually be wasted.

We are also making interesting developments in using bacteria for extraction. Using the latest genetic

modification techniques we have developed a new strain of bacteria that can separate copper from copper

sulfide at twice the speed of unmodified bacteria. In the future it should also be possible to use this

technology to extract a range of other metals.

a)   Why do you think the company is keen to develop a way of
extracting copper from waste material?

....

....

b)   Explain why using bacteria to extract copper from ores is more environmentally friendly than
electrolysis.

....

....

Metals from Rocks

Q4 This table shows some common **metal ores** and their formulas.

Ore	Formula
Haematite	Fe_2O_3
Magnetite	Fe_3O_4
Pyrites	FeS_2
Galena	PbS
Bauxite	Al_2O_3

Name the two elements that are commonly bonded to metals in ores.

....

Q5 **Gold** is often extracted from ores that contain very **small** percentages of the metal, but iron is only extracted from ores with a **large** percentage of the metal. Explain why.

....

....

Q6 New mines always have **social**, **economic** and **environmental** consequences. Complete this table to show the effects that a new mine can have.

Remember to include both positive and negative effects.

Social	Economic	Environmental
Services, e.g. healthcare may be improved because of influx of people.		Pollution from traffic.

Top Tips: Remember that metals are finite resources — there's a set amount on Earth and once we've extracted them all there won't be any more. We need to be able to get metals out of low-grade ores (ones that only contain small amounts of metal) to get enough to go round.

The Reactivity Series

Q1 If zinc is heated with copper oxide this reaction happens:

zinc + copper oxide → copper + zinc oxide

a) Why does this reaction take place? ....

b) Would it be possible to produce zinc oxide by reacting zinc with aluminium oxide? ....

Explain your answer. ....

Q2 One of the first metals to be extracted from its ore was **copper**. The discovery may have happened when someone accidentally dropped some copper ore into a wood fire. When the ashes were cleared away some copper was left.

a) What was the source of carbon in the fire?

....

b) Why do you think that copper was one of the first metals to be extracted from its ore?

....

c) Many metals, like potassium and magnesium, were not discovered until the early 1800s. What had to be developed before they could be extracted?

How are they extracted?

....

Q3 Fill in the blanks in this passage:

.... can be used to extract metals that are ....

it in the reactivity series. Oxygen is removed from the metal oxide in a

process called .... Other metals have to be extracted using

.... because they are .... reactive.

Q4 Imagine that four new metals, **antium**, **bodium**, **candium** and **dekium** have recently been discovered. Bodium displaces antium but not candium or dekium. Dekium displaces all the others. Put the new metals into their order of reactivity, from the most to the least reactive.

....

Top Tips: Stuff on the reactivity series isn't easy, so don't worry too much if you found these questions difficult. You don't need to learn the reactivity series off by heart, so spend plenty of time making sure that you understand reduction, electrolysis and displacement reactions.

Making Metals More Useful

Q1   Most iron is made into the alloy **steel**.

a)   Write a definition of the term '**alloy**'.

....

....

b)   How is **iron** turned into **steel**?

....

....

Tonight Matthew, I'm going to be... steel.

Q2   Draw lines to connect the correct phrases in each column.
One has been done for you.

Metal / Alloy	What has been added	Use
low-carbon steel	nothing	blades for tools
iron from a blast furnace	chromium	cutlery
high-carbon steel	0.1% carbon	car bodies
stainless steel	1.5% carbon	ornamental railings

Q3   Complete the following sentences using the metals below.

gold   copper   silver   nickel   titanium

a)   Bronze is an alloy that contains ....

b)   Cupronickel, which is used in 'silver' coins, contains copper and ....

c)   To make gold hard enough for jewellery it is mixed with metals such as ....

Chemistry 1a — Products from Rocks

Making Metals More Useful

Q4 Draw a diagram showing the structure of **iron**. Annotate your diagram to explain why iron and other metals can be **bent** and **shaped** without breaking.

Q5 24-carat gold is **pure** gold. 9-carat gold contains **9 parts** gold to 15 parts other metals. 9-carat gold is **harder** and **cheaper** than 24-carat gold.

  a) What percentage of 9-carat gold is actually gold?

....

  b) Why is 9-carat gold harder than pure gold?

....

....

Q6 Recently, scientists have been developing **smart alloys** with **shape memory** properties.

  a) Give an example of a use for smart alloys.

....

Smart Alloy of the Month Award

Presented to: _Nitinol_

Presented by: _CGP_

  b) What **advantages** do smart alloys have over ordinary metals?

....

....

  c) Give **two disadvantages** of using smart alloys.

....

....

Top Tips: As you must know by now, metals have lots of pretty useful properties, but they can be made even more useful by being mixed together to make alloys. Smart alloys are great for making those bendy glasses that don't break when you sit on them.

More About Metals

Q1 a) Aluminium and titanium are similar in some ways but different in others.
Complete this table to compare the properties of aluminium with those of titanium.

Property	Aluminium	Titanium
Density	low	low
Reactivity		
Strength		
Corrosion resistance	high	high
Cost		

b) What **properties** of **titanium** make it particularly useful for making **artificial hip joints**?

....

Q2 Aluminium and titanium are both described as **corrosion resistant**.
If you put a small piece of each metal into a beaker of dilute, hot **hydrochloric acid** nothing will
happen for several minutes. Then the **aluminium** will start to bubble quickly and dissolve.
The **titanium** will not change. Explain why the two metals behave like this.

....

....

....

Q3 Wherever possible, every scrap of gold is **recycled**. We also recycle **aluminium** as
much as possible, even though it is the most common metal in the Earth's crust.
Explain the reasons why we **recycle** these two metals.

....

....

....

Top Tips: Well, I hope you've had fun on this metals extravaganza. The good news is that
none of this is too complicated — just make sure you've learnt the properties of the everyday metals
like iron, aluminium and titanium and why they're so useful.

Fractional Distillation of Crude Oil

Q1   Circle the correct words to complete these sentences.

    a)   Crude oil is a **mixture** / **compound** of different molecules.

    b)   The molecules in crude oil **are** / **aren't** chemically bonded to each other.

    c)   If crude oil were heated the **first** / **last** thing to boil off would be bitumen.

    d)   Diesel has **larger** / **smaller** molecules than petrol.

Q2   Label this diagram of a **fractionating column** to show where these substances can be collected.

petrol   kerosene   diesel   oil   bitumen

These are in order of smallest to largest molecules from left to right.

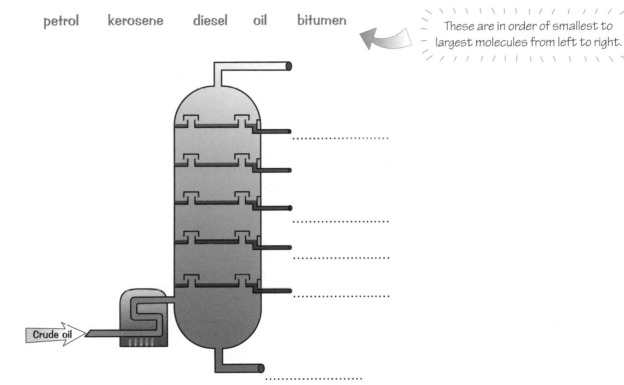

Q3   What is the connection between the **size** of the **molecules** in crude oil and their **condensing** (or **boiling**) points?

....

....

Q4   The fractional distillation of crude oil is described as a **continuous process**. What does this mean?

....

....

Properties and Uses of Crude Oil

Q1   Crude oil is a mixture of **hydrocarbons**. These **hydrocarbons** are mostly **alkanes**.

a)   Draw the structures of the first four **alkanes** and name each alkane you have drawn.

b)   Which of the alkanes you have drawn would you expect to have the highest boiling point?

....

Q2   There are some basic **trends** in the way that **alkanes** behave.
Circle the correct words to complete these sentences.

a)   The longer the alkane molecule the more / less viscous (gloopy) it is.

b)   The shorter the alkane molecule the more / less volatile it is.

c)   A very volatile liquid is one with a low / high boiling point.

Q3 a)   What is the **general formula** for **alkanes**?

> If you can't remember it you can work it out by looking at the diagrams you have drawn at the top of the page.

....

b)   **Eicosane** is a hydrocarbon that can be used to make candles. Each molecule of eicosane contains **20 carbon** atoms. What is the **chemical formula** for eicosane?

....

Q4   Each hydrocarbon molecule in engine oil has a **long** string of carbon atoms.

a)   Explain why this type of oil is good for using as a **lubricant** in an engine.

....

b)   Engines get very **hot** when they are in use. Why would oil molecules with **short** carbon chains be unsuitable for use as lubricants?

....

....

Using Crude Oil as a Fuel

Q1 Crude oil **fractions** are often used as **fuels**.

Remember fuels aren't just used in vehicles.

Give **four** examples of fuels that are made from crude oil.

....

Q2 As crude oil is a **non-renewable** resource people are keen to find **alternative** energy sources. Suggest a problem with each of these ways of using alternative fuels.

a) **Solar** energy for cars: ....

b) **Wind** energy to power an oven: ....

c) **Nuclear** energy for buses: ....

Q3 Using oil products as fuels causes some **environmental** problems.
Explain the environmental problems that are associated with each of the following:

a) **Transporting** crude oil across the sea in tankers.

....

b) **Burning** oil products to release the energy they contain.

....

Q4 Forty years ago some scientists predicted that there would be no oil left by the year 2000, but obviously they were **wrong**. One reason is that modern engines are more **efficient** than ones in the past, so they use less fuel. Give two other reasons why the scientists' prediction was wrong.

....

....

Q5 Write a short paragraph summarising why crude oil is the most **common source** of fuel even though **alternatives** are available.

....

....

....

74

Environmental Problems

Q1 Draw lines to link the correct parts of these sentences.

The main cause of acid rain is   acid rain.

Acid rain kills trees and   sulfuric acid.

Limestone buildings and
statues are affected by   acidifies lakes.

In clouds sulfur dioxide
reacts with water to make   sulfur dioxide.

Q2 Give **three** ways that the amount of **acid rain** can be reduced.

....

....

....

Q3 a) Write a word equation for completely **burning** a **hydrocarbon** in the open air.

....

b) Write **balanced symbol equations** for completely burning these alkanes in open air:

i) Methane: ....

ii) Propane: ....

Q4 **Exhaust** fumes from cars and lorries often contain **carbon monoxide** and **carbon particles**.

a) Why are they more likely to be formed in **engines** than if the fuel was burnt in the open air?

....

b) Why is carbon monoxide **dangerous**?

....

Top Tips: The best way to prevent acid rain damage is to reduce the amount of sulfur dioxide that we release into the atmosphere. When acid rain does fall there are some ways of reducing the amount of damage it causes, such as adding powdered limestone to affected lakes.

Chemistry 1a — Products from Rocks

Environmental Problems

Q5 Look at the graph and then answer the questions below.

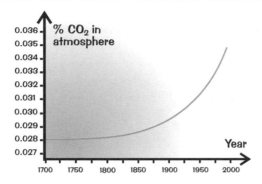

a) Describe the **trend** shown by the graph.

....

b) What is the main cause of this trend?

....

c) What effect do many scientists believe the trend shown in the graph is having on the Earth's average temperature?

....

Q6 **Hydrogen** is often talked about as the 'fuel of the future'.

a) What is the **only product** produced when **hydrogen** is burned?

....

b) Why is it better for the **environment** if we burn hydrogen rather than petrol?

....

c) Currently, most of the vehicles that can use hydrogen as a fuel are demonstration vehicles that are being developed by scientists. Explain the problems that will have to be overcome before the public will be able to use hydrogen-powered vehicles on a large scale.

....

Think about storage of hydrogen and the costs involved.

....

....

Top Tips: Scientists are constantly looking at the ways people are damaging the environment and trying to come up with ways of reducing the damage. But different scientists have different opinions on issues like global warming and they don't all agree about what should be done.

Chemistry 1a — Products from Rocks

Environmental Problems

Q7   In Brazil **ethanol** produced by **fermenting** sugar cane is a popular fuel for vehicles. The ethanol is mixed with **petrol** before it is used.

a)   What products are produced when **ethanol** (C_2H_5OH) is completely burnt?

....

b)   Why is ethanol made in this way a **carbon neutral** fuel?

....

Q8   **Biogas** is a mixture of **methane** (CH_4) and **carbon dioxide**. It is produced by microorganisms digesting waste material.

a)   What products are formed when **biogas** is burnt?

....

b)   What would be the main problem with using a **biogas generator** in Iceland?

....

Q9   Scientists are working hard to develop new **technologies** that are **environmentally friendly**.

a)   Summarise the developments in technology in these areas that are helping to reduce environmental damage:

i) Sulfur emissions from power stations ....

....

ii) Carbon dioxide emissions from vehicles ....

....

b)   List some ways that people can alter their lifestyles so that they cause less environmental damage.

....

....

c)   Do you think it is solely the responsibility of scientists to find ways of reducing environmental damage or should people be prepared to change their lifestyles too? Explain your answer.

....

....

....

Mixed Questions — Chemistry 1a

Q1 Metals make up about 80% of all the elements in the periodic table.

a) Shade the area where **metals** are found on this periodic table:

b) Read each of the following statements about metals. If the statement is true, tick the box.

☐ Metals are generally strong but also malleable.

☐ Metals are shiny when freshly cut or polished.

☐ Metal atoms are held together with ionic bonds.

☐ Generally, metals have low melting and boiling points.

☐ Properties of a metal can be altered by mixing it with another metal to form an alloy.

c) Metals are good electrical conductors. Explain why this is the case.
You should use ideas about **structure** and **bonding** in your answer.

....

....

....

d) Look at the information in the table below. R, S, T and U are all metals.
Explain in detail which material would be most suitable to build an **aeroplane body**.

Material	Strength	Cost (£)	Density (g/cm³)	Melting Point (°C)
R	High	100	3	1000
S	Medium	90	5	150
T	High	450	8	1200
U	Low	200	11	1070

....

....

....

Q2 The extraction, transportation and processing of crude oil is a major industry.

a) Name one product of the crude oil industry, other than a fuel.

....

b) Name one problem associated with the **transportation** of crude oil.

....

Mixed Questions — Chemistry 1a

Q3 The metals **aluminium**, **copper** and **iron** can be extracted from their **ores**.

a) Metal ores are often described as 'finite resources'. Explain the term '**finite resource**'.

....

b) The table shows the **reactivity series** of metals and **dates of discovery**.

i) What pattern can be seen in the data?

....

....

ii) Suggest an explanation for this.

....

....

....

metal	discovery	
potassium	AD 1807	most reactive
sodium	AD 1807	
calcium	AD 1808	
magnesium	AD 1755	
aluminium	AD 1825	
carbon		
zinc	about AD 1400	
iron	about 2500 BC	
tin	about 2000 BC	
lead	about 3500 BC	
hydrogen		
copper	about 4200 BC	
silver	about 4000 BC	
gold	about 6000 BC	
platinum	before 1500 BC	least reactive

c) Complete the following table by adding the **name** of a common ore of each metal and its **formula**.

metal	name of ore	chemical formula of ore
iron	haematite	
aluminium		
copper		

d) **i)** Complete the word equation for the reduction of iron ore with carbon monoxide.

iron(III) oxide + ... → **iron** + ...

ii) Write a **balanced symbol equation** for this reaction. (The formula of iron(III) oxide is Fe_2O_3.)

....

e) Copper metal can be extracted from its ore by **reduction** using carbon then purified by **electrolysis**.

i) Explain why electrolysis is used to produce copper metal for **electrical wiring**.

....

ii) Give **two** physical properties of copper that make it suitable for use in **electrical wiring**.

1...

2...

f) One of the most common elements present in the Earth's crust is aluminium.
Explain why aluminium metal can only be extracted using **electrolysis**.

....

....

Mixed Questions — Chemistry 1a

Q4   **Petrol** and **diesel** are two commonly used fuels for cars.

a)   Diesel has longer molecules than petrol.
List **four** differences you would expect in physical properties between petrol and diesel.

1. ....

2. ....

3. ....

4. ....

b)   **Ethanol** is an alternative fuel to petrol and diesel.

i)   How can ethanol be produced? ....

ii) Why is ethanol a more environmentally friendly fuel?

....

Q5   **Lubricating oils** in car engines keep moving metal surfaces apart. Viscous oils do this better than runny oils, but if they're too viscous they don't lubricate the moving parts properly.

The following experiment was set up to find which of two oils was the more viscous.
The time taken for each oil to run through the burette was noted at two temperatures.

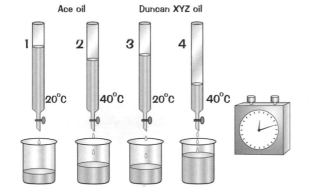

Burette	Temperature (°C)	Time for 50 cm³ of oil to flow through (s)
1	20	90
2	40	53
3	20	64
4	40	28

Use the table of results to answer the following questions:

a)   Which oil is **more viscous** at 20 °C? ....

b)   Temperatures in an engine are much higher than 40 °C.
What will happen to the viscosity of these oils at engine temperature?

....

c)   How could you **improve** the experiment to find out which oil would be more viscous when used in an engine?

....

d)   Which oil would you expect to be tapped off closer to the top of a fractionating column?

....

Mixed Questions — Chemistry 1a

Q6   Calcium carbonate ($CaCO_3$), in the form of the rock **limestone**, is one of the most important raw materials for the chemical and construction industries.

a)   Limestone can be processed to form **slaked lime**.

i)   Complete the flow diagram.

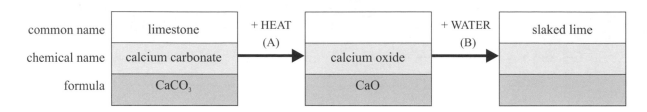

common name	limestone	+ HEAT (A)	calcium oxide	+ WATER (B)	slaked lime
chemical name	calcium carbonate				
formula	$CaCO_3$		CaO		

ii)   Write a balanced symbol equation for reaction A.

.... → .... + ...

iii)   Give one use of slaked lime.

....

b)   Limestone can be processed to form useful building materials. Complete the flow diagram.

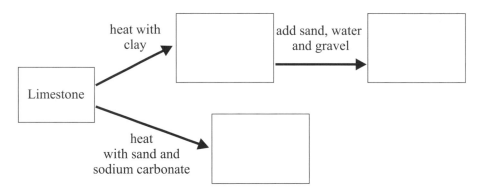

heat with clay

add sand, water and gravel

Limestone

heat with sand and sodium carbonate

c)   Give **two** reasons why limestone is more likely to be used as a building material than **wood**.

1.

2.

d)   Limestone is also used in the manufacture of **glass**.

i)   Name the other two main ingredients of glass.

....

ii)   By what simple process are these ingredients turned into glass?

....

e)   The limestone of the Houses of Parliament is crumbling away.

What is causing the damage to the limestone and how?

....

Chemistry 1a — Products from Rocks

Cracking Crude Oil

Q1   Fill in the gaps with the words below.

high	shorter	long	catalyst	cracking	diesel	molecules	petrol

There is more need for .... chain fractions of crude oil such

as .... than for longer chains such as ....

Heating .... hydrocarbon molecules to ....

temperatures with a .... breaks them down into smaller

.... This is called ....

Q2   Diesel is **cracked** to produce products that are more in demand.

a)   Suggest three useful substances that are produced when diesel is cracked.

....

b)   Write down a reason why long hydrocarbons do not make good fuels.

....

c)   What type of reaction is cracking? ....

Q3   After cracking both **alkenes** and **alkanes** are present.

a)   Bromine water is used to test whether a substance is an alkane or alkene.
Alkenes decolourise bromine water, but alkanes don't.

Which of the following would decolourise bromine water?

☐ propane   ☐ ethane   ☐ ethene

*Alkanes end with -ane,
alkenes end with -ene.*

b)   Put the steps of the cracking process in the correct order by writing numbers in the boxes.

☐ The vapour is passed over a catalyst at a high temperature.

☐ The long-chain molecules are heated.

☐ The molecules are cracked on the surface of the catalyst.

☐ They are vaporised (turned into a gas).

Q4   Change this diagram into a **word equation** and a **symbol equation**.

a)   Word equation: .... → .... + ...

b)   Symbol equation: .... → .... + ...

Alkenes and Ethanol

Q1 Complete this table showing the molecular and displayed formulas of some alkenes.

Alkene	Formula	Displayed formula
Ethene	a)	b)
c)	C_3H_6	d)
Butene	C_4H_8	e)

There are 2 different forms of butene — draw both.

Q2 The general formula for alkenes is C_nH_{2n}. Use it to write down the formulas of these alkenes.

a) pentene (5 carbons) ....

b) hexene (6 carbons) ....

c) octene (8 carbons) ....

d) dodecene (12 carbons) ....

Q3 True or false?

		True	False
a)	Alkenes have double bonds between the hydrogen atoms.	☐	☐
b)	Alkenes are unsaturated.	☐	☐
c)	Alkenes are not very useful.	☐	☐
d)	Ethene has two carbon atoms.	☐	☐

Q4 There are two ways of making ethanol:

A Sugar → ethanol + carbon dioxide   **B** Ethene + steam → ethanol

a) Which of the word equations describes making ethanol by **fermentation**? ....

b) Ethanol can be used as a fuel. In some countries the fermentation method is often used to produce it. Give two reasons why this method is chosen.

1. ....

2. ....

c) Give a disadvantage of the fermentation method.

....

d) What conditions are needed to make ethanol from ethene and steam?

....

....

Using Alkenes to Make Polymers

Q1 Tick the box next to the **true** statement below.

☐ The monomer of poly(ethene) is ethene.

☐ The polymer of poly(ethene) is ethane.

☐ The monomer of poly(ethene) is ethane.

We bring you gold, frankincense...
and poly-myrrh

Q2 **Low density poly(ethene)** and **high density poly(ethene)** are both made from the same monomers, but have very different properties.

a) Explain what causes the different properties.

....

....

b) Poly(styrene) and poly(propene) have different properties. Why is this likely to be?

....

....

Q3 Most polymers are **not** biodegradable.

Biodegradable means that something can rot.

a) What problems does this cause for the environment?

....

....

b) How can you minimise this environmental problem when using objects made from polymers?

....

....

c) Things are often made from plastics because they are cheap. Why might this change in the future?

....

....

Using Alkenes to Make Polymers

Q4   The equation below shows the polymerisation of ethene to form **poly**(ethene).

$$n \begin{pmatrix} \text{H} & \text{H} \\ | & | \\ \text{C} = \text{C} \\ | & | \\ \text{H} & \text{H} \end{pmatrix} \longrightarrow \begin{pmatrix} \text{H} & \text{H} \\ | & | \\ \text{C} - \text{C} \\ | & | \\ \text{H} & \text{H} \end{pmatrix}_n$$

many ethene
molecules

poly(ethene)

Draw a similar equation below to show the polymerisation of propene (C_3H_6).

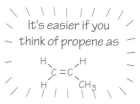

It's easier if you think of propene as

Q5   Fractional distillation of crude oil produces useful fractions and not-so-useful fractions.
The not-so-useful ones are **cracked** to form alkenes. Alkenes can be **polymerised** to make plastics.

Write down the differences between cracking and polymerisation.

....

....

....

Q6   Harvey makes two samples of slime by mixing poly(ethenol) with sodium tetraborate.
The slime samples are made with two **different concentrations** of sodium tetraborate solution.

Harvey places a ball of each slime sample in the centre of a circular disc and times how
long it takes for the samples to flow to the outside of the disc. His results are shown below.

Sample	Time (seconds)
A	14
B	31

a) Which slime sample was made from the strongest solution of
sodium tetraborate? Explain your answer.

....

....

b) Suggest one thing that Harvey should have kept the same to make it a fair test.

....

Top Tips: It's amazingly easy to name polymers. You just take the name of the monomer
(the little molecules that are joined together) stick it in brackets, and write the word 'poly' in front of it.
And Bob's your uncle (except if his name's Mike or anything else that's not Bob).

Plant Oils and Emulsions

Q1 Oil can be extracted from some **fruits** and **seeds**.

a) Name two fruits and two seeds which are good sources of oil.

Fruits: .... and ....

Seeds: .... and ....

b) Give two uses of plant oils. ....

c) Why is the use of **high pressure** an important part of the oil extraction process?

....

d) **Centrifugation** is the high speed spinning of a material. Why is it often used in oil extraction?

....

Q2 Each of these sentences has an error. Write out a **correct version** of each sentence.

a) Vegetable oils provide loads of energy, but are not nutritious.

....

b) Emulsions are always formed from oil suspended in water.

....

c) The thicker an emulsion, the less oil it contains.

....

d) Emulsions can be combined with air, but it makes them runnier.

....

Air is whipped into cream to make a topping for a trifle.

e) Emulsions are only found in foods.

....

Q3 Milk and cream are both **oil-in-water emulsions**.
They have different properties because of their different compositions.

In the boxes below draw diagrams to show the composition of the
oil-in-water emulsions **milk**, **single cream** and **double cream**.

Milk	Single cream	Double cream

Extracting and Using Plant Oils

Q1   Vegetable oils can be turned into fuels.

a)   Name two vegetable oils that can be turned into fuels.

.... and ....

b)   Why are vegetable oils suitable for processing into fuels?

....

Q2   Biodiesel is a fuel made from vegetable oil.
A litre of biodiesel contains **90%** of the energy found in a litre of normal diesel.

Normal diesel contains 37 megajoules (37 000 000 J) of energy per litre.
How much energy does a litre of biodiesel contain?

....

Q3   Biodiesel is more environmentally friendly than normal diesel or petrol.
However, it is unlikely to replace them in the near future.

a)   Give three reasons why biodiesel is more environmentally friendly than petrol or normal diesel.

1.   ....

2.   ....

3.   ....

b)   Explain why biodiesel is unlikely to replace petrol or normal diesel in the near future.

....

c)   Give two advantages that biodiesel has over other "green" car fuels such as biogas.

1.   ....

2.   ....

Q4   Biodiesel is said to be "**carbon neutral**".

a)   Explain why this is.

....

....

b)   Why is normal diesel not carbon neutral?

....

....

Extracting and Using Plant Oils

Q5 Read this passage and answer the questions below.

Biodiesel is a liquid fuel which can be made from vegetable oils. It's renewable, and can be used instead of ordinary diesel in cars and lorries. It can also be blended with normal diesel — this is common in some countries, such as France. You don't have to modify your car's engine to use biodiesel.

Biodiesel has several advantages. Producing and using it releases 80% less carbon dioxide overall than producing and using fossil-fuel diesel. So if we want to do something about climate change, using biodiesel would be a good start. Biodiesel is also less harmful if it's accidentally spilled, because it's readily biodegradable.

In the UK, we make most of our biodiesel from recycled cooking oils. But we don't make very much yet — you can only buy it from about 100 filling stations. The Government has been making some effort to encourage us to use more biodiesel. There's one major problem — it's about twice as expensive to make as ordinary diesel.

Most of the price you pay for petrol or diesel is not the cost of the fuel — it's tax, which goes straight to the Government. Over the last decade, the Government has increased fuel taxes, making petrol and diesel more expensive to buy. Part of the reason they've done this is to try to put us off buying them — because burning fossil fuels releases harmful pollutants and contributes to climate change.

So, to make biodiesel cheaper, in 2002, the Government cut the tax rate on it. The tax on biodiesel is now 20p/litre less than it is on normal diesel. This makes biodiesel a similar price to normal diesel. If the Government cuts the tax even further, then more people would be keen to use biodiesel, and more filling stations would start to sell it.

Pay less tax — buy biodiesel

a) In the UK, what do we produce most of our biodiesel from at present?

b) What would the environmental impact be if biodiesel was more widely used?

c) What has the Government done to encourage people to switch from normal diesel to biodiesel?

d) If lots more people start buying biodiesel instead of normal diesel, what problem is this likely to cause for the Government?

e) "I don't want to change to biodiesel. I don't want all the hassle of getting my car modified, and biodiesel costs more. It's just another way for the Government to get money off the taxpayers."

Write a response to this using information from the passage above.

Using Plant Oils

Q1   Ben and Martin both planned an experiment to identify saturated and unsaturated oils.

Ben's Method	Martin's Method
1. Put some oil in a test tube.	1. Put 2 ml of oil into a test tube.
2. Add some bromine water.	2. Label the test tube with the name of the oil sample.
3. Shake vigorously.	3. Add 5 drops of bromine water.
4. Repeat for next oil.	4. Record any colour change.
5. When all the oils are done, write down the results.	5. Repeat for each oil.

Whose experimental method is better? Give reasons for your answer.

....

....

Q2   Match each label below to a fatty acid structure.

Saturated animal fat

Polyunsaturated grape seed oil

Monounsaturated olive oil

Q3   Margarine is usually made from partially hydrogenated vegetable oil.

a)   Describe the process of hydrogenation.

....

....

b)   How does hydrogenation affect the melting points of vegetable oils?

....

Q4   Some types of fats are considered bad for your heart.

a)   Explain why saturated fats are bad for your heart.

....

....

b)   Partially hydrogenated vegetable oil contains **trans fats**. What effect do these have on the blood?

....

....

Food Additives

Q1 Food colourings are usually made up of several different dyes. These can be separated out.

a) What is the name of the **separation** technique that allows us to examine the dyes used in foods?

....

b) Which dye is **more soluble**, A or B? ....

c) Which would travel more slowly, a **more soluble** or a **less soluble** dye?

....

Mmmm... E507, my favourite.

Q2 Fill in the gaps in the passage using the words below. Use each word only once.

additives	compounds	appearance	ingredients	salt	approved
longer	chemical	preserve	taste	E-numbers	sodium sorbate

Nowadays there are a variety of ways to .... food, such as refrigeration, canning or pickling. One of the biggest advances has come through the use of ....

Using .... to preserve food is not a new idea.

For hundreds of years people have been using .... to keep food fresh for .... Scientists have used this basic idea to develop a number of different additives that not only preserve food, but can alter other characteristics of foods, such as the texture, the .... or the ....

Most additives used in the UK have .... For example, the preservative .... is E201. These are chemical compounds which have been .... for use in Europe. The additives must be listed in the .... on the packaging.

Top Tips: Additives with E-numbers aren't always the evil things you might be led to believe they are. Take E300 for instance — it's ascorbic acid and stops food going off as quickly. It sounds very unnatural and you might think that it's bound to be bad for you. But it's actually just vitamin C.

Food Additives

Q3   Jacob did a chromatography experiment and got the following results.

a) Write a brief method for this experiment, describing what Jacob would have done.

Colour of Sweet	Distance Travelled by Dye (mm)		
Brown	10	17	18
Red	18		
Green	10	17	
Orange	10	18	26
Blue	5	17	

....

....

....

....

....

b) How many dyes do the results indicate that the blue sweet contains? ....

c) Which sweet might contain the same mix of dyes as the red and green sweets together? Give a reason for your answer.

....

....

Q4   "I try to avoid eating all additives. I don't want to put those unnatural chemicals into my body." Write a response to this statement using your knowledge about additives.

....

....

....

Q5   Use the ingredients list from a bottle of orange squash to answer the questions below.

Orange Squash
Water
Comminuted orange from concentrate (10%)
Citric acid
Acidity regulator (sodium citrate)
Flavourings
Sweeteners (aspartame, sodium saccharin)
Stabiliser (carboxymethylcellulose)
Preservative (potassium sorbate)
Colour (beta-carotene)

a) What is the main ingredient in the squash?

....

b) Why have flavourings and colourings been added to the orange squash?

....

....

c) Do you think this product would be suitable for someone with diabetes? Explain your answer.

....

d) Name an additive that has been added to stop the ingredients from separating.

....

Plate Tectonics

Q1 Below is a letter that Alfred Wegener might have written to a newspaper explaining his ideas. Use your knowledge to fill in the gaps.

Dear Herr Schmidt,

I must reply to your highly flawed article of March 23rd 1915 by telling you of my theory of .... Finally I can explain why the .... of identical plants and animals have been found in seemingly unconnected places such as .... and ....

The current idea of sunken .... between these continents is complete hogwash. I propose that South America and South Africa were once part of a much larger land mass that I have named .... This supercontinent has slowly been drifting apart over millions of years. The pieces are being pushed by tidal forces and the .... of the Earth itself.

I will shortly be publishing a full report of my scientific findings.

Yours faithfully,

A Wegener

Q2 True or false?

	True	False
Wegener found that each continent had its own unrelated collection of plant and animal fossils.	☐	☐
Animals were thought to have crossed between continents using land bridges.	☐	☐
The Earth's continents seem to fit together like a big jigsaw.	☐	☐
Rocks are made of layers, which are different on every continent.	☐	☐
Fossils of tropical plants have been found in places where they shouldn't have survived, like the Arctic.	☐	☐
Pangaea is thought to have existed 3 million years ago.	☐	☐
Most scientists immediately agreed with Wegener's ideas.	☐	☐
Wegener had a PhD in geology.	☐	☐
Investigations of the ocean floor showed that although Wegener wasn't absolutely right, his ideas were pretty close.	☐	☐
Wegener died before his ideas were accepted.	☐	☐

Plate Tectonics

Q3   Wegener's theory of continental drift was put forward after he found **evidence**.
List four pieces of evidence that Wegener found.

1. ....
....

2. ....
....

3. ....
....

4. ....

....

....

Q4   According to Wegener's theory, the continents were moving apart.

a) **i)** What two forces did Wegener suggest were responsible for the movement of the continents?

....

ii) Why did many scientists say that this was impossible?

....

iii) Give two other reasons why most scientists weren't convinced by Wegener's theory.

....

....

b) Where did scientists finally find evidence that supported Wegener's ideas?

....

....

The Earth's Structure

Q1 Look at the diagram showing the boundary between the African and Arabian plates.

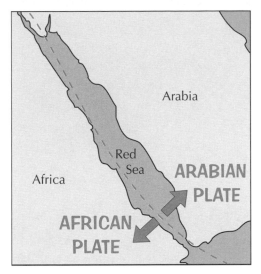

The Red Sea is widening at a speed of 1.6 cm per year.

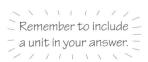
Remember to include a unit in your answer.

a) If the sea level remains the same, how much will the Red Sea widen in 10 000 years?

....

b) The Red Sea is currently exactly 325 km wide at a certain point. If the sea level remains the same, how wide will the Red Sea be at this point in 20 000 years' time?

....

....

Don't forget to make sure your distances are in the same unit.

Q2 The map below on the left shows where most of the world's earthquakes take place.

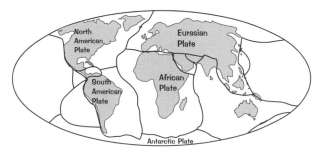

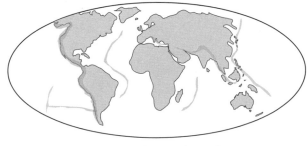 = main earthquake zones

Compare this map to one showing the tectonic plates.
What do you notice about the main earthquake zones?

....

....

The Earth's Structure

Q3 Draw a simple diagram of the Earth's structure.
Label the crust, mantle and core and write a brief description of each.

Q4 Match up the description to the key phrase or word.

| Crust | Hot spots that often sit on plate boundaries |

| Mantle | A well-known plate boundary in North America |

| Convection current | Caused by sudden movements of plates |

| Tectonic plates | Thinnest of the Earth's layers |

| Eurasian Plate | Caused by radioactive decay in the mantle |

| Earthquakes | Large pieces of crust and upper mantle |

| Volcanoes | Slowly flowing semi-solid layer that plates float on |

| San Andreas Fault | Moving away from the North American Plate but toward the African Plate |

Q5 How do scientists predict volcanic eruptions and earthquakes?
Complete the table to show what **evidence** can be collected, and comment on its **reliability**.

	Evidence	How reliable is it?
Earthquake		
Volcanic eruption		

Top Tips: That's the problem with "evidence" predicting earthquakes and volcanic eruptions — it's nowhere near 100% reliable. There are likely to be shed-loads of people living near a volcano or on a fault line — it'd be impossible to evacuate them all every time scientists thought there might possibly be an eruption or an earthquake some time soon — it just wouldn't work.

The Evolution of the Atmosphere

Q1 Tick the boxes next to the sentences below that are **true**.

When the Earth was formed, its surface was molten. ☐

The Earth's early atmosphere is thought to have been mostly oxygen. ☐

When oxygen started building up in the atmosphere, all organisms began to thrive. ☐

When some plants died and were buried under layers of sediment, the carbon they had removed from the atmosphere became locked up as fossil fuels. ☐

The development of the ozone layer meant the Earth's temperature reached a suitable level for complex organisms like us to evolve. ☐

Q2 The amount of **carbon dioxide** in the atmosphere has changed over the last 4.5 billion or so years.

Describe how the level of carbon dioxide has changed and explain why this change happened.

....

....

....

....

Q3 Draw lines to put the statements in the **right order** on the timeline. One is done for you.

Present

NOT TO SCALE

4600 million years ago

Don't get confused — 4600 million is the same as 4.6 billion.

The Earth cooled down slightly. A thin crust formed.

Water vapour condensed to form oceans.

The Earth formed. There was lots of volcanic activity.

More complex organisms evolved.

Plant life appeared.

The atmosphere is about four-fifths nitrogen and one-fifth oxygen.

Oxygen built up due to photosynthesis, and the ozone layer developed.

Chemistry 16 — Oils, Earth and Atmosphere

The Evolution of the Atmosphere

Q4   The pie chart below shows the proportions of different gases in the Earth's atmosphere today.

a)   Add the labels '**Nitrogen**', '**Oxygen**', and '**Carbon dioxide and other gases**'.

Earth's Atmosphere Today

Water vapour

b)   Give the approximate percentages of the following gases in the air today:

Nitrogen ....

Oxygen ....

c)   This pie chart shows the proportions of different gases that we think were in the Earth's atmosphere 4500 million years ago.

Earth's Atmosphere 4500 Million Years Ago

Carbon dioxide

Nitrogen

Other gases

Water vapour

Describe the main differences between today's atmosphere and the atmosphere 4500 million years ago.

....

....

d)   Explain why the amount of water vapour has decreased.

....

What did the water vapour change into?

....

e)   Explain how oxygen was introduced into the atmosphere.

....

f)   What were two effects of the rising oxygen levels in the atmosphere?

1.   ....

....

2.   ....

....

Chemistry 1b — Oils, Earth and Atmosphere

The Evolution of the Atmosphere

Q5 Noble gases are found in our atmosphere.

a) Name the six noble gases.

....

b) In which group of the periodic table are they found? ....

c) What is special about these gases?

....

d) What percentage of our atmosphere do the noble gases make up?

....

e) Write down a use for each of the following noble gases.

Argon: ....

Neon: ....

Helium: ....

Q6 There is a scientific theory that says that the water on Earth came from comets, not volcanoes.

Why is this theory not accepted by many scientists?

....

Think of different types of water.

....

Q7 Scientists now have evidence that the ozone layer is thinning and in places holes have developed. This has been linked to an increase in skin cancer over the past 30 years.

a) Explain why the thinning of the ozone layer is thought to have contributed to the rise in skin cancer.

....

....

b) Do these facts prove that the thinning of the ozone layer has caused the rise in skin cancer cases? Explain your answer.

....

....

Top Tips: Don't jump to conclusions — always look at evidence suspiciously. Think about what else might have caused the effect. Take skin cancer for example — it's increased over the last 30 years, during which time the ozone layer has been thinning. But this doesn't mean that there's definitely a link. There have been lots of lifestyle changes too, and some of these may be responsible.

Chemistry 1b — Oils, Earth and Atmosphere

98

The Evolution of the Atmosphere

Q8   Answer these questions about the damage to the ozone layer.

a)   Over which areas of the Earth have holes in the ozone layer occurred?

....

b)   Which gases were the main cause of the holes?

....

c)   Name two household products which contained these gases.

....

Q9   The graphs below show the changes in atmospheric carbon dioxide levels and temperature since 1850.

a) **i)**   Name two human activities that are thought to have contributed to the rise in carbon dioxide levels over the last 150 years.

   1. ....

   2. ....

  ii)   Do all scientists agree that the increase in carbon dioxide concentration has definitely been caused by these human activities? If not, explain the scientists' reasons.

   ....

   ....

b) **i)**   Look at the temperature graph.
           Has the temperature increased or decreased as carbon dioxide has risen?

   ....

  ii)   Many scientists believe that the temperature has changed because there is more carbon dioxide to trap the Sun's energy. What name is given to gases which trap heat from the Sun?

   ....

Chemistry 1b — Oils, Earth and Atmosphere

Mixed Questions — Chemistry 1b

Q1 The general formula for an alkene is C_nH_{2n}.

a) **Explain** what this general formula means. ....

....

b) The structural formula for ethene is shown to the right.
Draw the structural formula for pentene in the other box.

c) How do alk**e**nes differ from alk**a**nes?

Ethene	Pentene
H H $\;\;\;C = C$ H H	

....

....

Q2 Octane is heated and passed over a catalyst.
It **thermally decomposes** as shown to the right.

octane → hexane + ethene

a) What is the process of splitting up long-chain hydrocarbons by thermal decomposition called?

....

b) **Decane** ($C_{10}H_{22}$) is cracked to produce **propene**.
Write a word equation and a symbol equation to show this.

word equation: ....

symbol equation: ....

c) Describe how ethene can be used to make **ethanol**.

....

d) Suggest **one** other way to make ethanol. What is the advantage of making it this way?

....

....

Q3 Ethene molecules can join together in a **polymerisation** reaction.

a) **Explain** the term '**polymerisation**'.

....

....

b) Styrene molecules can also join together to form a polymer.
Name this polymer and **draw** a diagram of part of it below.

....

Styrene
H H $\;\;\;C = C$ H ⬡

c) **Plastics** are polymers. Most plastics aren't biodegradable. Explain one problem this creates.

....

Mixed Questions — Chemistry 1b

Q4 The **ingredients** list from a tin of **macaroni cheese** is shown below.

> **Macaroni Cheese — Ingredients**
> Water, Durum Wheat, Cheddar Cheese, Rapeseed Oil, Salt, Sugar,
> Skimmed Milk Powder, Mustard, Stabilisers (Polyphosphates,
> Sodium Phosphate), Flavour Enhancer (E621), Colour (E160)

Another situation where stabilisers would have held everything together.

a) **i)** Explain why E160 has been added to the macaroni cheese.

....

ii) A food magazine reported that two readers suffered headaches after eating the macaroni cheese. They concluded that additives such as E160 are harmful to health. Discuss whether this conclusion is valid.

....

....

b) **i)** Which ingredient in the macaroni cheese is likely to contain the most saturated fat?

....

Animal products tend to contain more saturated fat.

ii) Name a **health problem** that too much saturated fat can cause?

....

c) **i)** The macaroni cheese contains rapeseed oil, which is a vegetable oil. It is mostly a monounsaturated oil. What does the term "**monounsaturated**" mean?

....

ii) Circle the correct word or words to complete this sentence.

Rapeseed oil will / will not **decolourise bromine water.**

iii) Vegetable oils can be mixed with water to form **emulsions**. Give two examples of foods that contain emulsions.

....

Q5 People used to think that the Earth's surface was all one piece. Today, we think it's made up of **separate plates** of rock.

a) It wasn't until the 1960s that geologists were convinced that this was the case. Suggest why there was little evidence to support the theory before the 1960s.

....

....

b) What is thought to cause the **movement** of the plates?

....

c) Name **two** kinds of natural disasters that can occur at the boundaries between plates.

.... and ....

Mixed Questions — Chemistry 1b

Q6 The graphs below give information about the Earth's atmosphere millions of years ago and today.

No one is certain about the exact composition of the early atmosphere so these figures are rough estimates.

a) Could the early atmosphere **support life** as we know it? Explain your answer.

....

....

b) Which **organisms** caused an increase in oxygen and a decrease in carbon dioxide?

....

c) Even though the level of **carbon dioxide** is much lower now than millions of years ago, in the last 250 years the level has **increased**. Complete the following passage by circling the correct words.

> Humans are increasing / decreasing the amount of carbon dioxide / oxygen in the
>
> atmosphere by burning / creating fossil fuels. Also, deforestation reduces / increases the
>
> amount of carbon dioxide absorbed / released from the atmosphere.

d) **i)** **Biodiesel** is a renewable fuel. What is it made from? ....

ii) Explain why burning biodiesel produces **no net increase** in atmospheric carbon dioxide.

....

....

iii) Give one reason why biodiesel isn't widely used at the moment.

....

e) Tick the correct boxes to indicate whether each statement is **true** or **false**.

	True	False
i) 5% of the atmosphere is noble gases.	☐	☐
ii) The amount of ozone in the ozone layer is decreasing.	☐	☐
iii) Very early in Earth's history volcanoes gave out gases.	☐	☐
iv) Scientists are good at predicting volcanoes and earthquakes.	☐	☐

Physics 1a — Energy and Electricity

Heat Transfer

Q1 a) Indicate whether each of the following statements is true or false.

True   False

i)   Heat radiation is sometimes called infrared radiation. ☐ ☐

ii) Conduction involves the transfer of energy between moving particles. ☐ ☐

iii) Hot objects do not absorb radiation. ☐ ☐

iv) Convection always involves a moving liquid or gas. ☐ ☐

v) Cold objects do not emit radiation. ☐ ☐

b) Write out corrected versions of the **false** statements.

....

....

....

Q2 Three flasks, each containing 100 ml of water, are placed in closed boxes. The water in the flasks and the air in the boxes are at different temperatures, as shown.

A Air in box 55°C — Water 60°C

B Air in box 50°C — Water 65°C

C Air in box 65°C — Water 70°C

Which flask will cool fastest?
Give a reason for your answer.

Flask .... will cool fastest because ....

....

Q3 Each sentence below contains two mistakes. Write out a correct version of each.

a) Infrared radiation is emitted from the centre of hot solid objects, but not from liquids or gases.

....

b) The fins on a motorcycle engine decrease the amount of radiation emitted and keep the engine warm.

....

....

Heat Transfer

Q4 Three pupils are talking about how we get heat energy from the Sun.

Peter:
The Sun warms the Earth by convection.

Lucy:
The Sun warms us because it is much hotter than the Earth.

Edmund:
If the Sun were bigger, it would give us more heat.

For each pupil, circle whether they are right or wrong, and explain your answer.

a) Peter is **right / wrong** because

....

b) Lucy is **right / wrong** because

....

c) Edmund is **right / wrong** because

....

Q5 Simon fills a shiny container with boiling water and measures its temperature every 5 minutes. The graph shows his results.

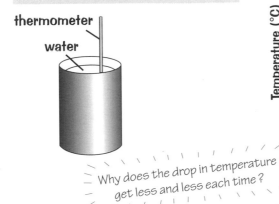

thermometer

water

Why does the drop in temperature get less and less each time?

a) Explain why the graph has this shape.

....

....

b) Simon's friend Jason repeats the experiment. He uses the same volume of boiling water in a can which is shallower and wider but otherwise identical.

Sketch on the graph above the results you would expect **Jason** to get.

Top Tips: Hot tea in a cold mug, surrounded by cold air, loses more heat to the mug (and air) than it absorbs from it. The greater the temperature difference, the faster your tea cools down.

Physics 1a — Energy and Electricity

Heat Radiation

Q1 Give a scientific reason why steel **electric kettles** are often made very **shiny**.

....

....

Q2 Tick the correct boxes below to show whether the sentences are true or false.

True **False**

a) The amount of heat radiation absorbed by a surface depends only on its colour. ☐ ☐

b) The hotter a surface is, the more heat it radiates. ☐ ☐

c) Good absorbers of heat are also good emitters of heat. ☐ ☐

d) Thermos flasks can keep hot things hot but cannot keep cold things cold. ☐ ☐

e) Silver survival blankets help the body to absorb heat. ☐ ☐

Q3 Ms Smith and Mr Jones each put a **solar hot water panel** on the roof of their houses.

Ms Smith's house

Mr Jones' house

Write down two reasons why Ms Smith gets more hot water than Mr Jones.

....

....

Q4 Complete the following sentences by circling the correct words.

a) Dark, matt surfaces are **good** / **poor** absorbers and **good** / **poor** emitters of heat radiation.

b) The best surfaces for radiating heat are **good** / **poor** absorbers and **good** / **poor** emitters.

c) The best materials for making survival blankets are **good** / **poor** absorbers and **good** / **poor** emitters.

d) The best surfaces for solar hot water panels are **good** / **poor** absorbers and **good** / **poor** emitters.

Physics 1a — Energy and Electricity

Heat Radiation

Q5 Tim did an investigation using a **Leslie's cube**.
Each surface on the cube had a different combination of **colour** and **texture**.

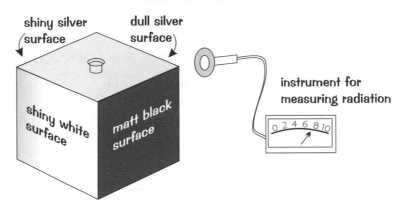

Tim measured the heat radiation coming from each surface. His results are shown below.

Surface	Reading	Colour and Texture
A	10	
B	4	dull silver
C	4	
D	2	

a) Complete the table to show which was:

i) the **matt black** surface.

ii) the **shiny silver** surface.

iii) the **shiny white** surface.

b) Tim's friend Julie copied his results for the experiment.
She then wrote a conclusion —

   "Dull silver and shiny white surfaces always emit the same amount of radiation."

Explain what is wrong with Julie's conclusion.

....

....

c) Which of the surfaces A to D would be best to use for the outside of a refrigerator?
Explain your answer.

....

....

Heat Conduction

Q1 Tick to show whether the sentences are true or false.

True **False**

a) Conduction involves **energy** passing between **vibrating particles**. ☐ ☐

b) Some **metals** are very **poor** conductors. ☐ ☐

c) **Solids** are usually better **conductors** of heat than liquids and gases. ☐ ☐

d) **Plastic** is a **poor** conductor because it contains **free electrons**. ☐ ☐

Q2 George picks up a piece of wood and a metal spoon. Both have the same temperature: 20 °C.

Explain why the metal spoon feels **colder** to the touch than the piece of wood.

....

....

Q3 In summer, Jamie wears a cotton vest.
In winter he wears a string vest.
He always wears the same kind of shirt.

Jamie's summer vest

Jamie's winter vest

Jamie finds that a string vest keeps him warmer than a cotton vest. Why is this?

....

....

Q4 Sajid, Mamphela and Ruth are discussing why copper is a good conductor of heat.

Sajid says, "**Copper is a great conductor because it's got electrons in it.**"

Mamphela says, "**It conducts well because it's shiny.**"

Ruth says, "**It conducts well because all its particles have kinetic energy.**"

Each pupil has made at least one mistake. Explain one mistake made by:

a) Sajid ....

....

b) Mamphela ....

....

c) Ruth ....

....

Physics 1a — Energy and Electricity

Heat Convection

Q1 a) Tick the sentences to show whether they are true or false.

True False

i) In a hot water tank, an immersion heater is usually placed
at the bottom of the tank. ☐ ☐

ii) The hotter the water, the denser it is. ☐ ☐

iii) Convection currents happen when hot water displaces cold water. ☐ ☐

iv) Convection currents can happen in water but not in air. ☐ ☐

b) Write a correction for each false sentence.

....

....

....

Q2 Tim tested a convector heater in three rooms.
The rooms all had the **same volume**, but they were **different shapes**.

Tall room

Cubic room

Long room

In which room would you expect the heater to work best? Explain your answer.

....

....

Q3 Match each observation with an explanation.

The very bottom of a hot water tank stays cold...

because water doesn't conduct much heat.

Warm air rises...

because heat flows from warm places to cooler ones.

A small heater can send heat all over a room...

because it is not so dense.

Heat Convection

Q4 Convection can make water flow round the pipes in a house, without using a pump. Miss Jenkins demonstrates this to her pupils using the apparatus below.

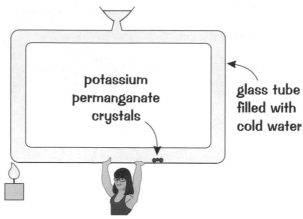

potassium permanganate crystals

glass tube filled with cold water

a) Draw arrows on the diagram to show which way the water moves.

b) Explain what happens to the water above the heat to cause the convection current.

....

....

....

....

....

Q5 Sam uses the apparatus shown to investigate heat transfer in water.

Ice floating at the top

Glass tube full of cold water

Ice weighted so it stays at the bottom

He heats the middle of the tube with a Bunsen flame. The ice at the top of the tube melts quickly, but the ice at the bottom does not melt.

What does this experiment show about conduction and convection in water? Explain your answer.

....

....

....

....

Top Tips: Remember, **convection** only happens in **fluids** (liquids and gases), **conduction** happens fastest in **solids**, but **all** objects emit and absorb heat **radiation**.

Useful Heat Transfers

Q1 List four features of a **Thermos flask** that reduce non-useful heat transfers.
State whether each reduces conduction, convection or radiation.

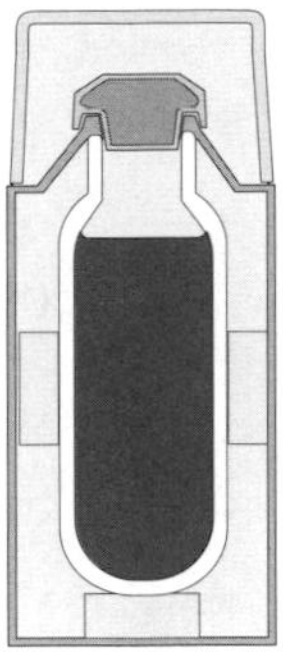

1. ....

2. ....

3. ....

4. ....

Q2 Natasha did an experiment to test how well plastic foam keeps a beaker of water hot.

She put different thicknesses of foam around three beakers.
The water in each beaker started off at 100 °C.

After 10 minutes Natasha read the temperatures. Her results are shown on the diagram below.

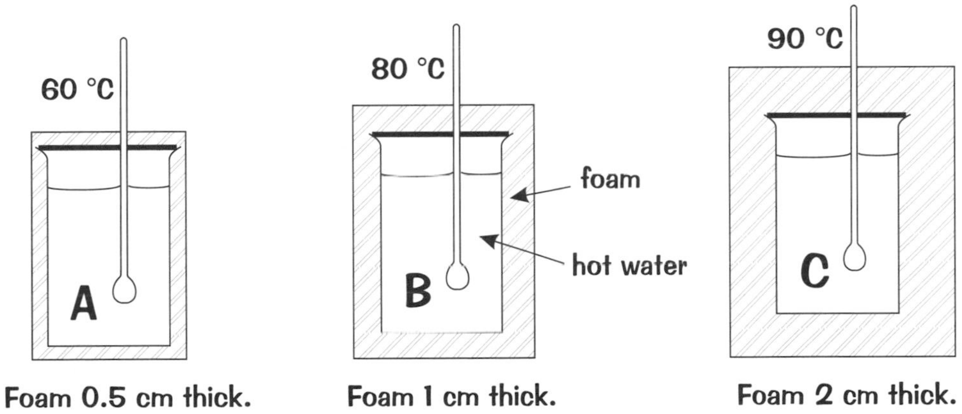

60 °C

80 °C

90 °C

foam

hot water

A

B

C

Foam 0.5 cm thick.

Foam 1 cm thick.

Foam 2 cm thick.

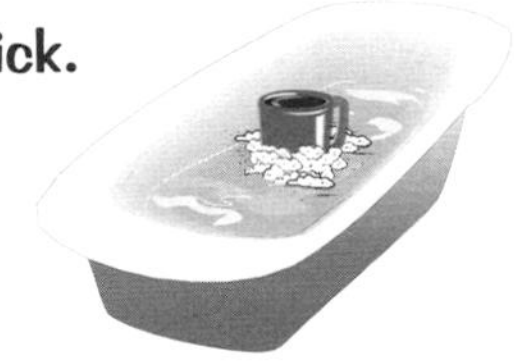

a) What do Natasha's results tell her?

....

....

b) In this experiment, what was: *This is the thing you measure.*

i) the dependent variable? ....

ii) the independent variable? ....   *This is the thing you change.*

c) Natasha's experiment does not include a **control** beaker.
What should she have used as a control, and how would this be useful?

....

....

Useful Heat Transfers

Q3 Mr Green makes a **solar hot water panel** from an old white central heating radiator made of **steel**.

Mr Green fixes the panel to the roof of his garden shed. Sadly, he finds that the water does not get very hot, even on sunny days.

Explain how Mr Green could improve the design of his solar hot water panel.

wooden support

old radiator

wooden roof

air space

pipes connected to hot water tank and pump

....

....

....

....

Q4 Mr Pink has a copper hot water tank with an electric **immersion heater** in it. The hot water tank **loses heat** from its **walls** by radiation, conduction and convection.

a) Describe one **useful** heat transfer that takes place in the hot water tank.

....

b) Complete the table below, showing how to **reduce non-useful** heat transfers from the tank's walls.

Type of Transfer	Suggested improvements to reduce heat loss
Radiation	
Conduction	
Convection	

Which fluid will move and carry heat away? Where will it go, and how could you stop it?

Top Tips: Clever people don't wear thick jumpers when it's cold out. Oh no. They put on two thinnish jumpers — to **trap air** between the layers and reduce their heat losses by convection and conduction. Then, they wrap themselves in tinfoil — to reduce their heat losses by radiation.

Energy Transfer

Q1 Complete the following **energy transfer diagrams**. The first one has been done for you.

A solar water heating panel: ....light energy........ → ....heat energy........

a) A gas cooker: .... → ....heat energy...........

b) An electric buzzer: ....electrical energy........ → ....

c) A television screen: .... → ....

Q2 Use the words below to fill in the gaps.

conservation   run out   stay the same   resources   principle

The word .... has two very different meanings related to energy.

It can mean using fewer energy .... so that they don't

.... It can also mean the .... that the total

amount of energy in the Universe will always ....

Q3 The diagram shows a **steam locomotive**.

a) What form(s) of energy are there in the:

i) coal ....

ii) hot steam (which powers the engine) ....

b) Describe two **energy transfers** which take place on the locomotive.

1. ....

2. ....

Q4 **Bruce is practising weightlifting.**

a) When Bruce holds the bar still, above his head, what kind of energy does the weight have?

....

b) Bruce had porridge for breakfast. Describe how the chemical energy in his porridge is converted to the gravitational potential energy of the lifted bar.

....

....

c) When Bruce lets go of the weight, what happens to its energy?

....

Efficiency of Machines

Q1 Fill in the gaps using the correct words from the list below.

| heat | light | input | create | output | total | useful | fraction | convert |

A **machine** is a device which can .... energy. Some of the energy

supplied to the machine is converted into .... output energy.

But some energy is always wasted — often as .... energy.

The **efficiency** of a **machine** is the .... of the **total energy**

.... that is converted into useful energy ....

Q2 Here is an **energy flow diagram** for an electric lamp. Complete the following sentences.

a) The **total energy input** is .... J

b) The **useful energy output** is .... J

c) The amount of energy **wasted** is .... J

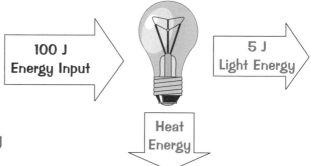

100 J Energy Input

5 J Light Energy

Heat Energy

Q3 Use the **efficiency formula** to complete the table.

Efficiency = Useful Energy Output ÷ Energy Input

Total Energy Input (J)	Useful Energy Output (J)	Efficiency
2000	1500	
	2000	0.50
4000		0.25
600	200	

Q4 Tina was investigating a model **winch** — a machine that uses an electric motor to lift objects.

Tina calculated that, in theory, **10 J** of electrical energy would be needed to lift a **boot** 50 cm off a table. She then tried lifting the boot with the winch, and found that, actually, **20 J** of electrical energy was used.

Why did the winch use so much electrical energy in practice?
In your answer, include an explanation of what happened to the 'extra' 10 joules.

....

....

Physics 1a — Energy and Electricity

Efficiency of Machines

Q5 Sajid hopes his new MP3 player is better than his old one. He decides to test which one is more **efficient**.

He puts new batteries in both MP3 players and switches them on. Then he times how long they each play for before the batteries run out.

a) Why does Sajid use new batteries?

....

b) How can he measure the **useful energy outputs**?

....

c) Write down one thing Sajid must do to make it a **fair test**.

....

d) Player A lasts for 3 hours and Player B lasts for 4 hours. Write a **conclusion** for Sajid's experiment.

....

Q6 Clive is researching different kinds of electric light bulb. He finds the following information.

	Low-energy bulb	Ordinary bulb
Electrical energy input per second (J)	15	60
Light energy output per second (J)	1.4	1.4
Cost	£3.50	50p
Typical expected lifetime	8 years	1 year
Estimated annual running cost	£1.00	£4.00

Hint — most people don't like wasting money.

a) Write down two reasons for choosing a **low-energy** light bulb.

1) ....

2) ....

b) Write down two reasons why Clive might prefer to buy an ordinary bulb.

1) ....

2) ....

Top Tips: There's often more to choosing a light bulb in real life. For example, you might put an ordinary bulb in a room you rarely use, because the running costs would be so tiny that any savings would never pay back the extra cost of buying a low-energy bulb.

Efficiency of Machines

Q7 Electric kettles have an **electric heater** which heats the water.
Mr and Mrs Bennett had an argument about their new electric kettle.

Mr Bennett says: "Electric heaters like this one are 100% efficient — they never waste energy."
Mrs Bennett says: "There are at least two ways this kettle could **waste** energy."

Say whether Mr and Mrs Bennett are **right** or **wrong** and explain why.

a) Mr Bennett is .... because ....

....

b) Mrs Bennett is .... because ....

....

Q8 True or false?

                                                                          True False

a) **i)** **Concentrated** energy is more **useful** than spread-out (or low-grade) energy. ☐ ☐

    ii) Whenever energy is transferred, some of it becomes less concentrated. ☐ ☐

    iii) Electric heaters can be 100% **efficient**. ☐ ☐

    iv) When energy is **transferred**, all the heat energy produced is always **wasted**. ☐ ☐

b) Write a correction for each false sentence.

....

....

....

Q9 Mrs Smith is choosing a new kettle.
She narrows the choice down
to the two kettles shown here.

3 litre stainless steel kettle **2 litre plastic kettle**

Write down five things Mrs Smith
should consider when she decides
which kettle to buy.

    1) ....

    2) ....

    3) ....

    4) ....

    5) ....

Energy Transformations

Q1 When an archer shoots an arrow into the air several **energy transformations** take place.
The table below shows these transformations, but in the wrong order.
Number the energy transformations from 1 to 5 to show the correct order.

Order	Energy transformation
	Energy stored in the pulled bow and string is converted into kinetic energy.
	The arrow loses gravitational potential energy and gains kinetic energy as it falls to earth.
	Chemical energy in the archer's muscles is converted into elastic potential energy.
1	Chemical energy from the archer's food is stored in his muscles.
	As it goes upwards the arrow loses kinetic energy and gains gravitational potential energy.

Q2 Sarah eats three slices of **toast and jam** before riding her bicycle to work. Describe the **energy transformations** that take place as Sarah cycles to work.

Don't forget about the energy that's wasted.

....

....

....

....

Q3 Each of the following sentences is incorrect. Write a correct version of each one.

a) In a battery-powered torch, the battery converts **electrical energy** into **light energy**.

....

b) A **wind turbine** converts **kinetic energy** into **electrical energy** only.

....

c) A wind-up toy car converts **chemical** energy into **kinetic energy** and **sound energy**.

....

Q4 Write down the name of a device which converts:

a) electrical energy into **sound energy** ....

b) light energy into **electrical energy** ....

c) electrical energy into **light energy** ....

Energy Transformation Diagrams

Q1   This diagram shows the energy changes in a **toy crane**. The diagram is drawn to scale.

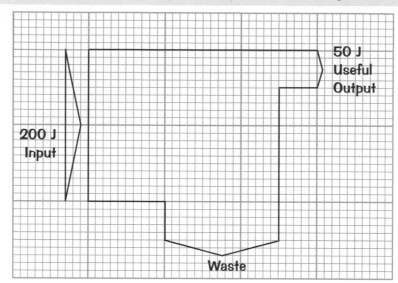

a)   How much energy is **one small square** worth?   .... J

b)   How much energy is **wasted**?   .... J

Q2   Professor Bean is testing a new **high-efficiency** car engine.
He finds that for every 100 J of energy supplied to the engine, 75 J are transformed into **kinetic energy** in the moving car, 5 J are wasted as **sound energy** and the rest is turned into **heat energy**.

On the graph paper below, draw an **energy transformation diagram** to illustrate his results.

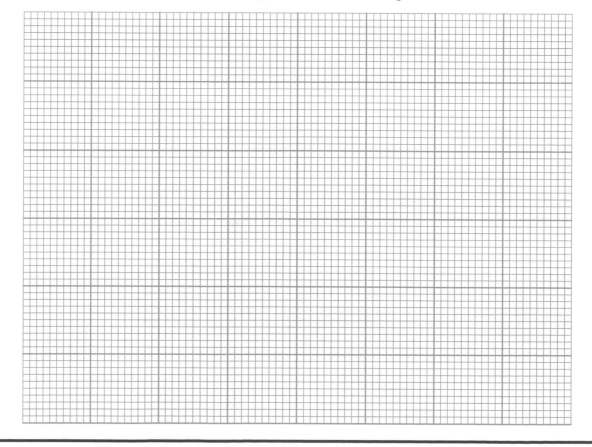

Energy Transformation Diagrams

Q3 Liam measured the energy input and outputs for a model **electrical generator**. He drew this diagram to show his results.

Describe two mistakes Liam has made on his diagram, and suggest how to correct them.

1. ....

....

....

2. ....

....

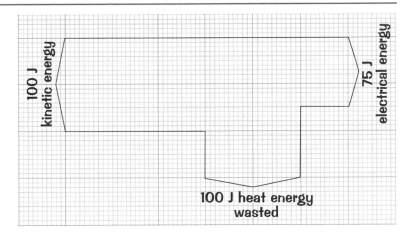

Q4 The Sankey diagram below is for a **winch** — a machine which **lifts** objects on hooks and cables.

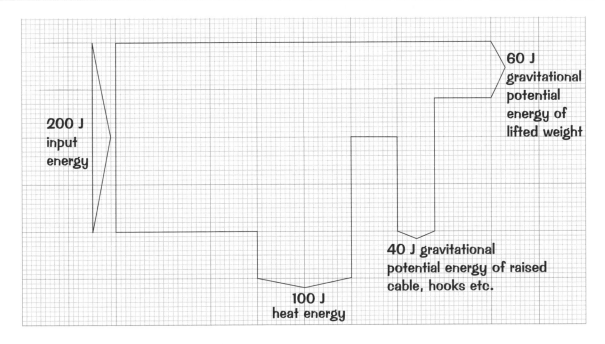

a) What is the total amount of energy **wasted**? .... J

b) How much useful **gravitational energy** is produced? .... J

c) Calculate the **efficiency** of the winch. Give your answer as a decimal.

Efficiency = Useful Energy Output ÷ Energy Input

....

....

Physics 1a — Energy and Electricity

The Cost of Electricity

Q1   Boris puts his **2 kW** electric heater on for 3 hours.

a)   Calculate how many **kilowatt-hours** of electrical energy the heater uses.

Energy used = ...

b)   Boris gets his electricity supply from Ivasparkco. They charge 7p per kilowatt-hour. Work out the **cost** of the energy calculated in part (a).

....

....

Q2   Calculate the cost of using a **100 W** lamp for **10 hours**, if electrical energy costs **11.3p per kWh**.

You need to turn 100 W into kilowatts first.

....

....

Q3   Tina's mum grumbles at her for leaving a 60 W lamp on overnight — about 9 hours every night. Tina says her mum uses **more energy** by using an 8 kW shower for 15 minutes every day.

Is Tina right? Calculate how much energy each person uses and compare your results.

....

....

....

....

Q4   Mr Havel recently received his electricity bill. Unfortunately, he tore off the bottom part to write a shopping list.

a)   How many **kWh** of energy did Mr Havel use in the three months from June to September?

....

b)   What would the bill have said for 'total cost'?

Customer : Havel, V	
Date	Meter Reading
11 06 06	34259
10 09 06	34783
Total Cost @ 9.7p per kWh	

....

....

Energy Efficiency in the Home

Q1 Heat is lost from a house through its **roof**, **walls**, **doors** and **windows**.

through the roof

through the walls

through the doors

....

....

....

....

....

....

a) In the spaces on the diagram, write down at least one measure that could be taken to reduce heat losses through each part of the house.

b) Miss Golightly has just bought a new house which has very large windows. Suggest three ways she could reduce heat loss through the windows of her new house.

1. ....

2. ....

3. ....

Q2 Explain how the following types of insulation work.

a) Cavity wall insulation ....

....

b) Loft insulation ....

....

c) Hot water tank jacket ....

....

Top Tips: If you want to build a new house, there are regulations about making it energy efficient — that's one reason why a lot of new houses have quite small windows. If you live in an old house, you can sometimes get a grant to cover the cost of installing extra insulation.

Energy Efficiency in the Home

Q3   Mr Tarantino wants to buy **double glazing** for his house, but the salesman tries to sell him insulated window shutters instead. He says it is cheaper and more **cost-effective**.

	Double glazing	Insulated window shutters
Initial Cost	£3000	£1200
Annual Saving	£60	£20
Payback time	50 years	

a)   Calculate the **payback time** for insulated shutters and write it in the table.

b)   Is the salesman's advice correct? Give reasons for your answer.

....

....

Q4   A **hot water tank jacket** and **thermostatic controls** do not directly prevent 'heat loss' from a house, but they **will** save energy (and therefore money).

a)   How can having **thermostatic controls** help to save energy?

....

b)   Explain how installing a **hot water tank jacket** would save you money.

....

Q5   Shona, Tim, Meena and Alison are discussing what 'cost-effectiveness' means.

Cost-effectiveness means having a short payback time.   **Shona**

Cost-effectiveness means getting good value for your money.   **Alison**

Cost-effectiveness means getting a job done for a low price.   **Tim**

Cost-effectiveness just means not wasting energy.   **Meena**

a)   Whose explanations do you think are right? Circle their names.

Shona   Alison   Tim   Meena

b)   Explain why the method with the shortest payback time is **not** always the best one to choose.

....

....

....

Electricity and the National Grid

Q1   Number these statements 1 to 5 to show the order of the steps that are needed
to deliver energy to Mrs Miggins' house so that she can boil the kettle.

	An electrical current flows through power cables across the country.
	Mrs Miggins boils the kettle for tea.
	Electrical energy is generated in power stations.
	The voltage of the supply is raised.
	The voltage of the supply is reduced.

Q2   Using **high voltages** in power cables means you need some **expensive** equipment.

  a)   Make a list of the main equipment you need for **high voltage transmission**.

....

....

  b)   Explain why it is still **cheaper** to use **high voltages** for transmission.

....

....

....

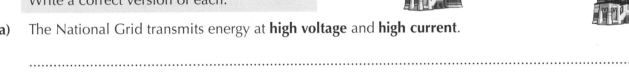

Q3   Each of the following sentences is incorrect.
Write a correct version of each.

  a)   The National Grid transmits energy at **high voltage** and **high current**.

....

  b)   Huge **insulators** are needed because the **cables** get so **hot**.

....

  c)   A step-up transformer is used to **reduce the voltage** of the supply before electricity is transmitted.

....

  d)   Using a **high current** makes sure there is not much energy **wasted**.

....

Top Tips: The National Grid's pretty good, really — we all get electrical energy whenever
we want it (mostly). The key thing to remember is the **high voltage**. And remember **why** it's used —
high voltage means low current, which means the cables don't get so hot — so less energy is **wasted**.

Non-renewable Energy & Power Stations

Q1   In a power station, there are several steps involved in making electricity.
Number these steps in the right order.

☐ Hot steam rushes through a turbine and makes it spin.

☐ Electricity is produced by the spinning generator.

☐ A fossil fuel such as coal is burned to release heat.

☐ The spinning turbine makes the generator spin too.

☐ Water is heated in a boiler and turned to steam.

Q2   Nuclear power stations provide about 20% of the UK's electrical energy.

a)   How do uranium and plutonium provide heat energy?

....

b)   Why is nuclear power so expensive?

....

....

Q3   Explain what 'non-renewable' means, in terms of energy resources.

....

Q4   Match up each environmental problem below with something that causes it.

| Acid rain | Releasing CO_2 by burning fossil fuels |

| Climate change | Coal mining |

| Dangerous radioactive waste | Sulfur dioxide formed by burning oil and coal |

| Spoiling of natural landscapes | Using nuclear power |

Q5   Lisa says: "Using nuclear power to make electricity is too dangerous."
Ben says: "Using fossil fuels is even more dangerous in the long run."

I ♥ NUCLEAR POWER

Say NO to Nuclear

Who do you think is right? Explain your answer.

....

....

....

Using Renewable Energy Resources (1)

Q1　Explain what 'renewable' means, in terms of energy resources.

....

Q2　People often object to wind turbines being put up near to where they live.

a)　List three reasons why they might object.

1) ....

2) ....

3) ....

b)　List three arguments in favour of using wind turbines to generate electricity.

1) ....

2) ....

3) ....

Q3　Geoff wanted to find out how much electricity he could generate using a small wind turbine. Each night he used a wind-powered generator to charge a battery. On each following day, he timed how long the battery could keep a lamp lit. His results are shown in the table below.

Day	Mon	Tues	Wed	Thu	Fri	Sat	Sun
Time lamp stays lit (mins)	45	50	2	25	60	35	42

a)　Why did Geoff time how long the lamp stayed lit?

....

b)　Suggest a reason why the lamp only stayed lit for 2 minutes on Wednesday.

....

Q4　Explain the advantages and disadvantages of using **solar cells** to generate electricity.

....

....

....

Using Renewable Energy Resources (2)

Q1   Lynn and Hua are using the apparatus below to investigate how hydroelectric power works.

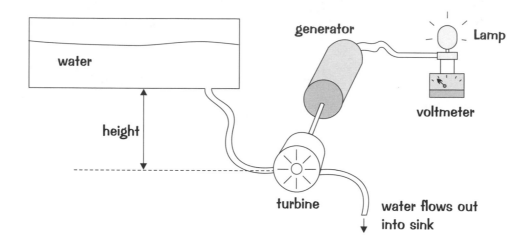

They put the tank at several different heights and recorded the voltage from the generator.

Height of tank (cm)	300	250	200	150	100
Voltage (V)	3.1	2.0	1.1	0.6	0.2
Brightness of lamp	bright	normal	dim	just lit	not lit

a)   Why did they measure the **voltage** instead of just noting the brightness of the lamp?

....

b)   They predicted that the energy generated would be **proportional** to the height of the tank.
Do their results support this prediction? Explain your answer.

Their results **support / do not support** their prediction because ....

....

c)   Why do you think the **voltage** was higher when the **tank** was higher?

....

Q2   These sentences explain how pumped storage works.
Put them in the right order by numbering them 1 to 4.

☐ Water at a high level stores energy until it is needed.

☐ At peak times, water is allowed to flow downhill, powering turbines and generating electricity.

☐ At night big power stations make more electricity than is needed.

☐ Spare electricity is used to pump water from reservoirs at a low level to others at a high level.

Using Renewable Energy Resources (2)

Q3 Match up the beginnings and ends of the sentences. In one case, two matches are possible.

Big coal-fired power stations deliver energy...

when it is needed.

Pumped storage power stations deliver energy...

all the time.

Hydroelectric power stations deliver electricity...

that they have previously stored.

Q4 At a public meeting, people are sharing their views about hydroelectric power.

We should use hydroelectric power more — it doesn't cause any pollution.

And it gives us loads of free energy.

But it makes a terrible mess of the countryside.

At least it's reliable — it always gives us electricity when we need it.

Brian **Hillary** **Sue** **Liz**

Say whether you agree or disagree with each person's view, and explain your reasons.

a) I **agree** / **disagree** with Brian because ....

....

b) I **agree** / **disagree** with Hillary because ....

....

c) I **agree** / **disagree** with Sue because ....

....

d) I **agree** / **disagree** with Liz because ....

....

e) Outline two **advantages** of hydroelectric power which were not mentioned at the public meeting.

 1) ....

 2) ....

f) Outline two **disadvantages** of hydroelectric power not mentioned at the meeting.

 1) ....

 2) ....

Using Renewable Energy Resources (3)

Q1 Tick the boxes to show whether each statement applies to **wave** power or **tidal** power or **both**.

Wave Tidal

a) Is usually used in estuaries. ☐ ☐

b) Suitable for small-scale use. ☐ ☐

c) Is a reliable way to generate electricity. ☐ ☐

d) The amount of energy generated depends on the weather. ☐ ☐

e) The amount of energy generated depends on the time of the month and year. ☐ ☐

Q2 **Tidal barrages** can be used to generate electricity.

What happens to make turbines go round?

a) Explain how a tidal barrage works.

....

....

....

b) Give two reasons why people might object to a tidal barrage being built.

1. ....

2. ....

Q3 **Wave-powered generators** can be very useful around islands, like Britain.

a) Number these sentences 1 to 6, to explain how a wave-powered generator works.

☐ The spinning generator makes electricity.

☐ The moving air makes the turbine spin.

☐ The water goes down again.

☐ Air is sucked downwards, spinning the turbine the other way and generating more power.

☐ A wave moves water upwards, forcing air out towards a turbine.

☐ The spinning turbine drives a generator.

b) Give two possible problems with using wave power.

1. ....

2. ....

Using Renewable Energy Resources (4)

Q1 Explain why:

a) Some rocks underground are very hot. ....

....

b) Biomass is a 'renewable' source of energy. ....

....

c) Burning biomass is 'carbon neutral'. ....

....

Q2 Mr Saleem is a cattle farmer in India. He has just installed a small **biogas** plant on his farm.

a) What source of biogas is Mr Saleem likely to use?

....

b) Apart from cooking and heating, how could Mr Saleem make use of the biogas?

....

Q3 Tick the correct boxes to show whether these statements apply to generating electricity from **geothermal** energy, **biomass** or **both**.

	Biomass	Geothermal
a) Set-up costs are low.	☐	☐
b) Does not release CO_2.	☐	☐
c) Possible in any country in the world.	☐	☐
d) Reduces the need for landfill sites.	☐	☐

Q4 Fiza and Julie are discussing the environmental impacts of burning landfill rubbish to generate electricity.

Fiza says: **"Burning rubbish gives off harmful gases."**

Julie says: **"But it's better than just burying your rubbish and burning coal instead."**

Who do you think is right? Explain your answer.

....

....

Top Tips: Burning animal poo is nothing new — people have been doing it for years, and many still do. For instance, if you're a nomadic yak herder in Mongolia, you probably don't have **mains electricity**, but you **do** have lots of **yak poo**. Dry it, burn it, and you'll have a nice warm tent.

Comparison of Energy Resources

Q1 The city of Fakeville decides to replace its old coal-fired power station. They have to choose between using gas, nuclear, wind or biomass.

Give one **disadvantage** of each choice:

a) **Gas** ....

....

b) **Nuclear** ....

....

c) **Wind** ....

....

d) **Biomass** ....

....

Q2 This is part of a leaflet produced by the pressure group 'Nuclear Is Not the Answer' (NINA).

Read the extract and answer the questions on the next page.

Imagine life without electricity. No lights, no computers, no TV… no kettles, no tea? Unthinkable. But that's what could happen when the oil and gas run out — because in the UK we generate about 80% of our electricity from power stations running on fossil fuels.

The Government is considering whether we should build more nuclear power stations. At NINA, we believe that nuclear is not the answer.

Nuclear power stations generate power, yes, but they also generate huge piles of highly radioactive waste. No one has any idea how to get rid of this waste safely. So should we really be making more of it? Radioactive waste stays dangerous for hundreds of thousands of years. Would you be happy living near a nuclear fuel dump? That's not all — nuclear power stations, and the lethal waste they create, are obvious targets for terrorists. And, last but not least, building more nuclear power stations would cost the taxpayer billions.

The good news is, we don't need nuclear power. There are safer, cleaner ways to produce electricity — using renewable energy. Many people argue that renewables are unreliable — the wind doesn't always blow, for instance. Well, true, but tidal power is reliable — and we have hundreds of miles of coastline with tides washing in and out twice every day.

There's still time. If you don't want your children to grow up in a nuclear-powered world, join NINA today.

Comparison of Energy Resources

a) Explain clearly why the author thinks that we could
find ourselves without electricity.

....

....

b) Give two reasons why the author thinks nuclear power is **dangerous**.

1. ....

....

2. ....

....

c) Apart from safety concerns, why else does the author feel that nuclear power is a bad choice?

....

d) The author suggests that tidal power is a **plentiful** and **reliable** source of energy.
Do you agree? Explain your answer.

I **agree** / **disagree** because

....

....

....

....

e) Give two possible arguments **in favour** of nuclear power.

1. ....

....

2. ....

....

Mixed Questions — Physics 1a

Q1 Explain:

a) how a layer of **snow** can stop young plants dying in the **frost**.

....

b) how cavity wall insulation works.

....

c) why birds try to keep warm in winter by **ruffling** up their feathers.

....

d) why, in winter, **cloudy** nights are usually **warmer** than clear nights.

....

....

Q2 Ben sets up an experiment as shown.
He records the temperature readings on thermometers A and B every two minutes.

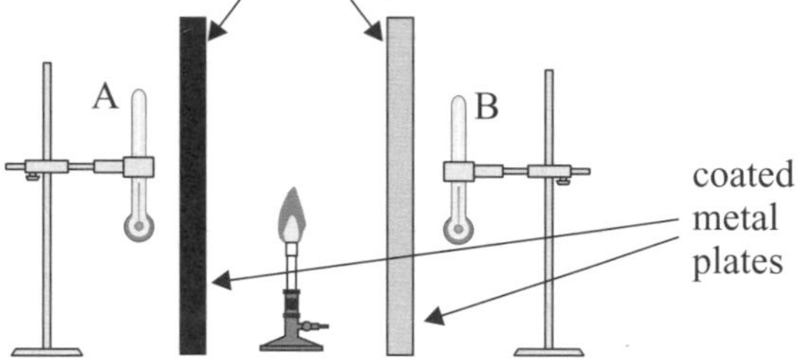

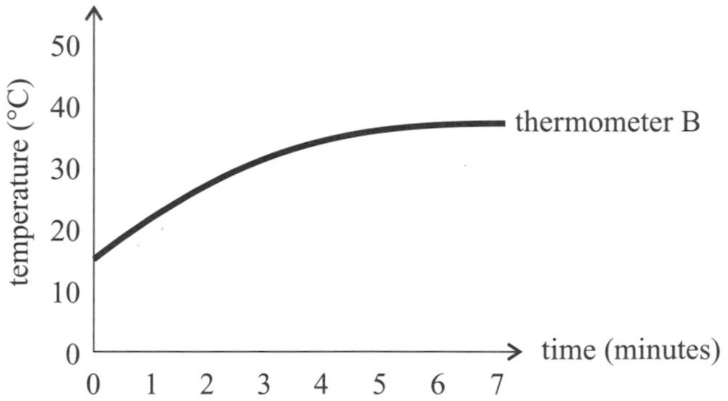

matt black surface
shiny silver surface
A
B
coated metal plates

The graph below shows Ben's results for thermometer **B**.

temperature (°C)
50
40
30
20
10
0
thermometer B
time (minutes)
0 1 2 3 4 5 6 7

a) On the diagram above, sketch the graph you would expect for thermometer **A**.

b) Explain why the differences between the two graphs occur.

....

....

Q3 Fridge-freezers often have their freezer compartment above the refrigerator.
How does this arrangement encourage **convection currents** in the main body of the fridge?

....

....

Mixed Questions — Physics 1a

Q4 Jemima is sanding some floorboards with an **electric sander** which has a power rating of **360 W**. Jemima has the sander on for **45 minutes**.

a) How many kWh of electrical energy does the sander use in this time?

....

b) If the sander is only **55% efficient**, how many **joules** of energy are **wasted**?

....

....

c) Jemima's electricity supplier charges **14.8p per kWh**. What will be the cost of the 'wasted' energy? (Give your answer to the nearest penny.)

....

Q5 In one gas-fired power station, for every **1000 J** of energy input to the power station, 100 J is wasted in the **boiler**, 500 J is wasted in the **cooling water** and 50 J is wasted in the **generator**.

a) What **type** of energy is contained in the **coal**? ....

b) On the grid below, draw a detailed energy transformation diagram for this power station.

c) Calculate the **efficiency** of the power station. ....

d) Electricity generated in power stations reaches our homes by a network of power cables. Explain:

   i) why these power cables are at very high voltages ....

   ....

   ii) why the high voltage is not dangerous for people using the electricity ....

   ....

Mixed Questions — Physics 1a

Q6   Eric investigates ways of saving energy in his grandmother's house. He calculates the annual savings that could be made on his grandma's fuel bills, and the cost of doing the work.

Work needed	Annual Saving (£)	Cost of work (£)
Hot water tank jacket	15	15
Draught-proofing	65	70
Cavity wall insulation	70	560
Thermostatic controls	25	120

a)   Which of these energy-saving measures has the shortest **payback time**?

....

b)   Which of the options in the table would save Eric's grandma the most money **over 5 years**? Show your working.

....

....

....

c)   Eric's grandma has an open fire which burns **logs**. Eric tells her this is an inefficient way to heat the house, and says she should have a **gas fire**. She says that burning natural gas is more environmentally damaging than burning logs. Is she right? Explain your answer.

....

....

....

Q7   A group of farmers live on a remote island, growing potatoes and farming llamas. They decide to put **solar cells** on the roofs of their houses and put up **wind turbines** in their fields.

a)   Suggest why the farmers have chosen to use:

i)   solar power   ....

....

ii) wind power   ....

....

b)   What other renewable sources of energy could the farmers use?

....

Electromagnetic Waves

Q1 Diagrams A, B and C represent electromagnetic waves.

A   **B**   **C**

a) Which two diagrams show waves with the same **frequency**? ...... and ......

b) Which two diagrams show waves with the same **amplitude**? ...... and ......

c) Which two diagrams show waves with the same **wavelength**? ...... and ......

Q2 Indicate whether the following statements are true or false.

True False

a) Visible light travels faster in a vacuum than both X-rays and radio waves. ☐ ☐

b) All EM waves transfer matter from place to place. ☐ ☐

c) Radio waves have the shortest wavelength of all EM waves. ☐ ☐

d) All EM waves can travel through space. ☐ ☐

Q3 Red and violet are at opposite ends of the spectrum of **visible** light.
Describe two things they have in common and two ways in which they differ.

....

....

....

....

Q4 EM waves with higher frequencies are generally more damaging. Explain, in terms of wavelength and frequency, why some **ultraviolet** radiation can be almost as damaging as **X-rays**.

....

....

Q5 **Green light** travels at 3×10^8 m/s and has a wavelength of about 5×10^{-7} m.

Calculate the **frequency** of green light. Give the correct unit in your answer.

You'll have to use $v = f\lambda$.

....

....

Electromagnetic Waves

Q6 The house shown below receives radio signals from a nearby transmitter, even though there is a mountain between the house and the transmitter.

radio transmitter

Use the words below to fill in the blanks in the passage.

ionosphere   direct current   short-wave   long-wave   alternating current   absorbs   reflects

The house can receive .... signals because they can bend

around the mountain. It also receives .... signals

because they are reflected by the .... A radio has an

aerial which .... the EM waves and changes them into an

....

Q7 The diagrams show the arrangement of atoms in a dense material and in a less dense material.

dense material
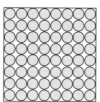

less dense material
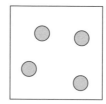

Dense materials are more likely to **reflect** or **absorb** electromagnetic waves. **Less dense** materials are more likely to transmit them.

Explain why this is.

Try drawing a ray of light hitting the material. How likely is it to hit an atom (and what happens to its energy when it does?)

....

....

....

Top Tips: **Absorption** of EM radiation can cause **heating** (useful in ovens) and/or an **alternating current** (useful in radios etc.). Radiation isn't always absorbed though — it could be reflected or transmitted. This depends on **what** the material is, and the **wavelength** of the radiation.

Electromagnetic Waves

Q8 Materials X, Y and Z were tested to see how well they transmit electromagnetic radiation. Detector B was used to measure what percentage of the energy emitted (from A) reached it.

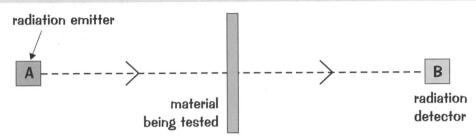

The table shows the results of the test.

Material	Detector B (%)
X	0
Y	90
Z	50

a) **i)** Which material **transmitted** most of the energy that was directed at it? ....

ii) What may have happened to the energy that was **not** detected at B when this material was tested?

....

....

b) **No energy** reached detector B when sample X was tested.
What conclusions can you draw from this result? Tick the boxes next to any valid conclusions.

☐ Sample X absorbed all the energy that was directed at it.

☐ Sample X reflected all the energy that was directed at it.

☐ Sample X would be a poor choice of material for using in windows

c) State **three** things which must be kept the same in this experiment to make it a fair test.

....

Q9 Indicate whether each statement is **true** or **false**.   **True False**

a) Some electromagnetic waves can kill cells in the body.   ☐   ☐

b) All electromagnetic waves are absorbed by the body.   ☐   ☐

c) The harm done by EM radiation depends on its wavelength (or frequency) only. ☐   ☐

Q10 Explain why:

a) Electric fires glow red, even though infrared radiation (heat radiation) is invisible to the human eye.

....

b) UV tubes glow blue, even though UV radiation is invisible to the human eye.

....

Microwaves and Infrared

Q1 Microwaves are used for **cooking** as well as for mobile phone **communications**.

Explain why your body does not get 'cooked' when you use a mobile phone.

....

....

Q2 Explain how a microwave camera on a remote-sensing satellite can 'see' through clouds.

....

....

Q3 Gabrielle in Britain and Carwyn in Canada are talking by mobile phone.

Communications Satellite

NOT TO SCALE

Carwyn's phone

Gabrielle's phone

Atlantic Ocean

a) The distance from phone to phone, via the satellite, is approximately 6000 km. How long will it take the signal from Gabrielle's phone to arrive at Carwyn's phone?

....

....

....

b) The signal from a mobile phone gets weaker with distance. How is this problem overcome?

....

....

c) Suggest why the satellite needs to be high above the Earth.

....

....

Microwaves and Infrared

Q4 A **cable TV** company uses a large dish to collect TV signals from a satellite in space. It then sends these signals to houses along **optical fibres**.

a) What type(s) of EM waves could be used to send the signals along the optical fibres?

....

b) Give three advantages of using optical fibres to transmit signals, rather than broadcasting them.

....

....

....

Q5 Doctors can use an **endoscope** to look inside a patient's body. An endoscope has two bundles of optical fibres — one carries light down into your stomach, say, and the other returns the reflected light back to a monitor.

Light source → Endoscope

a) What material could the optical fibres in the endoscope be made from?

....

b) Optical fibres work because of repeated **total internal reflections**.

i) Complete the ray diagrams below. The critical angle for glass/air is 42°.

air / glass   air / glass

You'll need to measure the angle of incidence for each one — carefully.

ii) What two conditions are essential for total internal reflection to occur?

....

....

c) Explain why doctors must be careful not to **bend** an endoscope sharply.

....

....

Microwaves and Infrared

Q6 Read this extract about the safety of microwave ovens.

Microwave ovens are designed to generate microwaves to heat up food. So should we be worried that microwaves are cooking us, as well as our dinner?

Well, probably not. The Microwave Technologies Association, which represents manufacturers, stresses that microwave ovens are lined with metal to stop microwaves getting out, and that there are regulations about how much 'leakage' is allowed. They also point out that the intensity of leaked radiation decreases rapidly with distance from the oven. So don't press your nose to the glass to watch your chicken korma reheating — gaze from a distance.

We can't be certain that microwave ovens are absolutely safe — there might be long-term health problems that no one's spotted yet. But perhaps we should be more worried about other uses of microwave technology, like mobile phones. Mobile phones use microwaves — though of a lower frequency than those used in ovens. But mobile phones are very definitely *designed* to emit microwaves (or else they wouldn't work) — so are they silently 'cooking' our brains?

Interestingly, my mobile phone can still make calls from inside a microwave oven, with the door shut. If the microwaves from my phone are powerful enough to get out of the oven — with all its fancy shielding — then what on earth are they doing to my brain?

a) Why might it be a serious health hazard if microwaves 'leak' from microwave ovens?

....

....

....

b) According to the article, microwave ovens have a **metal lining** to stop microwaves getting out. This suggests that microwaves may be (circle any which apply):

    A   absorbed by the metal lining

    B   reflected by the metal lining

    C   transmitted by the metal lining

Microwaves and Infrared

c) Why does the article advise you not to "press your nose to the glass" of a microwave oven?
Circle the correct answer.

    A   because the radiation from microwave ovens is known to cause cancer

    B   because some radiation may be "leaking" from the oven

    C   to avoid bruising

    D   because you might burn your skin

d) Why does keeping your distance from a microwave oven
reduce the chance that you will suffer harmful effects from it?

....

....

e) Why does the article mention that the Microwave Technologies Association represents
manufacturers?

....

....

f) Mobile phones also emit microwaves when you are making a call.

    i)   Do the microwaves emitted by **mobile phones** have a longer or shorter **wavelength**
than those used in ovens? Circle the correct answer.

               longer   shorter

    ii) Why does the author think we should be more concerned about the ill effects of microwaves
from mobile phones than from microwave ovens?

....

....

Top Tips: People love a good scare story. Microwave ovens are **probably** perfectly safe.
Mobile phones haven't been around for so long, so it's difficult to know if they're doing us any
long-term harm. You could say, though, that it's safer to stay at home, heating up ready meals in the
microwave and making calls on your mobile, than it is to cross a busy, fume-choked city street to
find a phone box or go to the pizza shop. Watch out for the salt in those ready meals, though.

Hazards of EM Radiation

Q1 Choose from the words below to complete this passage.

lead   plastic   bones   transmitted   soft tissue   aluminium   absorbed

X-rays can pass easily through .... but are ....

more by .... Screens and shields made of

.... are used to minimise unnecessary exposure to X-rays.

Q2 Give two examples of how EM waves can be **helpful** and two examples of how they can be **harmful**.

Helpful: 1) .... 2) ....

Harmful: 1) .... 2) ....

Q3 The graph opposite shows how the **energy** of EM waves varies with **frequency**.

a) What is the mathematical relationship between frequency and energy?

....

....

b) Draw arrows to match points **A**, **B** and **C** on the graph to the three types of radiation below.

| green light | gamma radiation | radio waves |

| A | B | C |

Q4 Explain why:

a) It is safe to use fluorescent tubes in lights, even though harmful UV rays are produced inside them.

....

b) Darker-skinned people are less likely to suffer from skin cancer.

....

....

c) Radiographers stand behind lead screens when they are taking X-rays of a patient, even though it's considered an acceptable risk for the patient to be deliberately exposed to X-rays.

....

....

Analogue and Digital Signals

Q1 Fill in the blanks, using the words below.

analogue	digital	analogue	amplified	weaken	interference	noise

All signals .... as they travel. To overcome this, they can be

.... Signals may also suffer .... from

other signals or from electrical disturbances. This causes ....

in the signal. When .... signals are amplified, the noise is

also amplified.

Q2 Sketch: a 'clean' digital signal.   a 'noisy' digital signal.   a 'noisy' analogue signal.

Q3 a) Explain why it is better to send **digital** signals to a computer rather than analogue ones.

....

b) Explain why digital signals suffer less from **noise** than analogue signals.

....

....

c) State one other advantage of using digital signals for communication.

....

Q4 The diagrams opposite show magnified views of the surfaces of a **compact disc** and an old-fashioned **record**.

The CD is 'read' by a laser, along the path shown by the arrow. The record is read by a needle which follows the grooves.

Both devices produce an electrical signal, which is then converted into sound.

For each device, sketch the type of trace you would expect to see on a monitor.

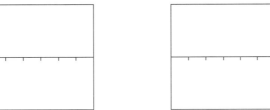

Compact disc   **Old-fashioned record**

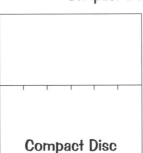

Compact Disc

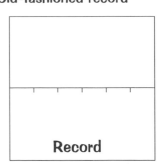

Record

Physics 1b — Radiation and the Universe

<u>Radioactivity</u>

Q1 Fill in the blanks using the words below. Each word should be used only once.

radiation isotope element protons neutrons nuclei radioactive

Isotopes are atoms which have the same number of ....

but different numbers of .... Some isotopes are

.... Their .... are unstable, so they

break down and spit out .... When this happens the

nucleus often changes into a new ....

Q2 Carbon-14 is radioactive but carbon-12 is not.
Explain why, in terms of the difference between their **nuclei**.

....

....

Q3 Indicate whether these sentences are **true** or **false**.

                                                  True False

a) The nucleus of an atom takes up almost no space compared to the whole atom. ☐ ☐

b) Most of an atom's mass is in the electrons. ☐ ☐

c) Atoms of the same element with the same number of neutrons are called isotopes. ☐ ☐

d) Radioactive decay speeds up at higher temperatures. ☐ ☐

Q4 In a famous experiment Sir Ernest Rutherford got his students
to aim a stream of **alpha particles** at a piece of **gold foil**.
They noticed that most of the particles went straight through,
unaffected in any way, but a few changed direction.

a) What had happened to the particles which changed direction?

....

....

b) What idea about the **nucleus** is supported by these results?

....

....

Radioactivity

Q5 Complete the passage using the words given below. You will not have to use all the words.

ions   less   more   electrons   further   less far   protons

When ionising radiation hits atoms it sometimes knocks ....

off the atoms and makes them into .... Radiations that are

more ionising travel .... into a material and tend to cause

.... damage in the material they have penetrated.

Q6 Complete the table below by choosing the correct word from each column.

Radiation Type	Ionising power weak/moderate/ strong	Charge positive/none/ negative	Relative mass no mass/ small/large	Penetrating power low/moderate/ high	Relative speed slow/fast/ very fast
alpha					
beta					
gamma					

Q7 a) For each sentence, tick the correct box to show whether it is **true** or **false**.

True **False**

i)   All nuclear radiation is deflected by magnetic fields. ☐ ☐

ii) Gamma radiation has no mass because it is an EM wave. ☐ ☐

iii) Alpha is the slowest and most strongly ionising type of radiation. ☐ ☐

iv) Beta particles are electrons, so they do not come from the nucleus. ☐ ☐

b) For each of the false sentences, write out a correct version.

....

....

....

144

Radioactivity

Q8 Radiation from three sources — A, B and C — was directed through an **electric field** (between X and Y), towards target sheets of **paper**, **aluminium** and **lead**. Counters were used to detect where radiation passed through the target sheets.

Source A — the radiation was partially absorbed by the lead.
Source B — the radiation was deflected by the electric field, and stopped by the paper.
Source C — the radiation was deflected by the electric field, and stopped by the aluminium.

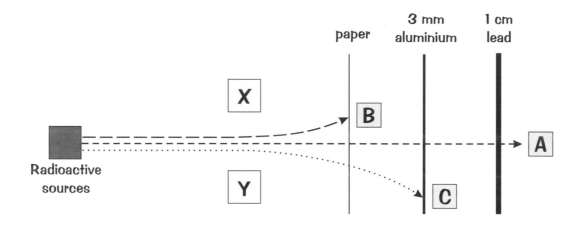

a) What type of radiation is emitted by:

source A? ...., source B? ...., source C? ....

b) Explain why source A is **not deflected** by the electric field.

....

....

c) What other type of **field** would deflect radiation from sources B and C? ....

Q9 Explain clearly why gamma rays are **less ionising** than alpha particles.

....

....

....

> **Top Tips:** Alpha, beta and gamma radiation are different **things** and they also have different **properties**. You need to understand how they vary in ionising power, penetrating power, speed etc.

Physics 1b — Radiation and the Universe

Half-life

Q1   A radioactive isotope has a half-life of 60 years.
Which of these statements describes this isotope correctly? Tick one box only.

In 60 years half of the atoms in the material will have gone. ☐

In 30 years' time only half the atoms will be radioactive. ☐

In 60 years' time the count rate will be half what it is now. ☐

In about 180 years there will be almost no radioactivity left in the material. ☐

Q2   The graph shows how the count rate of a radioactive isotope declines with time.

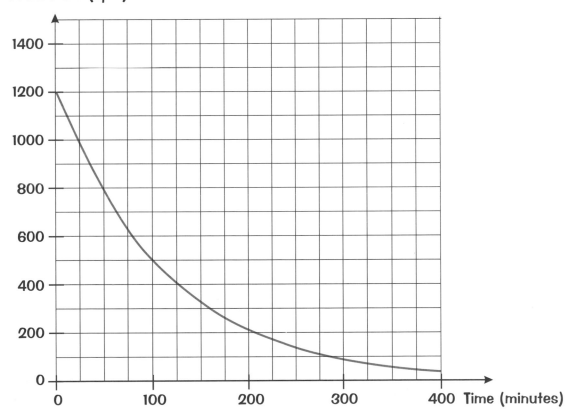

Count Rate (cpm)

a)   What is the half-life of this isotope? ....

b)   What was the count rate after 3 half-lives? ....

c)   What fraction of the original radioactive nuclei will still be unstable after 5 half-lives?

....

d)   After how long was the count rate down to 100? ....

Half-life

Q3 The half-life of uranium-238 is 4500 million years. The half-life of carbon-14 is 5730 years.

a) What do the '238' in "uranium-238" and the '14' in "carbon-14" mean?

....

....

b) If you start with a sample of each element and the two samples have equal activity, which will lose its radioactivity first? Circle the correct answer.

uranium-238   carbon-14

Q4 A radioactive isotope has a half-life of 40 seconds.

You'll need to change 6 minutes into seconds.

a) What fraction of the unstable nuclei will still be radioactive after 6 minutes?

....

....

b) **i)** If the initial count rate of the sample was 8000 counts per minute, what would be the approximate count rate after 6 minutes?

....

....

ii) After how many whole **minutes** would the count rate have fallen below 10 counts per minute?

....

....

Q5 Peter was trying to explain half-life to his little brother. He said, "isotopes with a long half-life are always more dangerous than those with a short half-life."

Is Peter right? Explain your answer.

....

....

....

Top Tips: Half-life tells you **how quickly** a source becomes **less radioactive**. If your source has a half-life of 50 years then after 100 years the count rate will be 1/4 of its original value. But if the half-life's 10 years, after 100 years the count rate will be less than 1/1000th of its original value.

Uses of Radiation

Q1 The table shows the **properties** needed for different uses of radioactivity, and the **types** of radioactive sources that are used.

Choose the appropriate words to complete the table (some have been done for you).

Use of radiation	Penetrating power (low/high)	Ionising power (low/high)	Half-life (short/long)	Type of radiation (α,β,γ)
Smoke alarm	Low			
Medical tracers			Short	
Detecting leaks in pipes		Low		

Q2 The following sentences explain how a smoke detector works, but they are in the wrong order.

Put them in order by labelling them 1 (first) to 6 (last).

☐ The circuit is broken so no current flows.

1 The radioactive source emits alpha particles.

☐ A current flows between the electrodes — the alarm stays off.

☐ The alarm sounds.

☐ The air between the electrodes is ionised by the alpha particles.

☐ A fire starts and smoke particles absorb the alpha radiation.

Q3 The diagram shows how radiation can be used to sterilise surgical instruments.

a) What kind of radioactive source is used, and why? In your answer, mention the **type** of radiation emitted (α, β and γ) and the **half-life** of the source.

....

....

b) What is the purpose of the thick lead?

....

c) Similar machines can be used to treat fruit before it is exported from South America to Europe, to stop it going bad on the long journey. How does irradiating the fruit help?

....

....

Uses of Radiation

Q4   Eviloilco knows that its oil pipeline is leaking somewhere between points A and B.

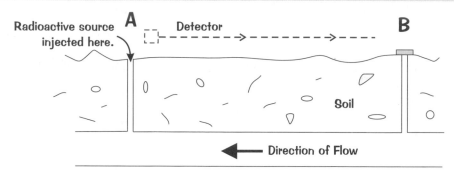

Radioactive source injected here.   **A**   Detector   **B**

Soil

← Direction of Flow

This is how Eviloilco plans to find the leak.

> **We will inject a source of alpha radiation into the pipeline at point A. (This source has a long half-life — giving us better value for money in the long term.) After injecting the radioactive material, we will pass a sensor along the surface above the pipeline — and so detect where radiation is escaping, hence pinpointing the leak.**

a)   Give **two** reasons why Eviloilco has made a bad choice of radioactive source, and describe the type of source they should use.

....

....

....

b)   Even if they use the correct type of radioactive source, their plan will still fail. Why?

....

Q5   A patient has a radioactive source injected into her body to test her kidneys.

A healthy kidney will get rid of the radioactive material quickly (to the bladder). Damaged kidneys take longer to do this.

The results of the test, for both the patient's kidneys, are shown opposite.

Kidney A

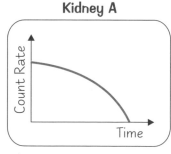

Kidney B

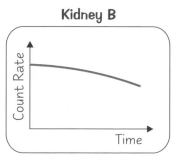

a)   Explain how the doctor knew which kidney was working well and which was not.

....

....

b)   Explain why an alpha source would **not** be suitable for this investigation.

....

....

Risks from Radiation

Q1   Two scientists are handling samples of radioactive material.

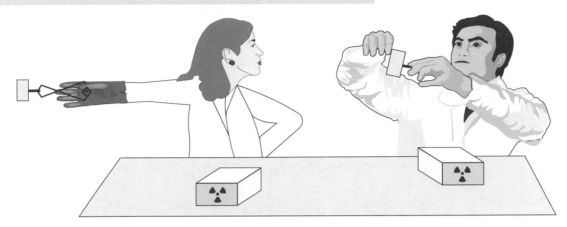

a)   One of the scientists is taking sensible safety precautions, but the other is not.
Describe three things which the careless scientist is doing wrong.

1.   ....

2.   ....

3.   ....

b)   Describe another way the scientists can reduce their exposure to the radiation,
without using special apparatus or clothing.

....

c)   How should radioactive samples be stored when they are not in use?

....

Q2   In industry, highly penetrating radiation sources sometimes need to be moved from place to place.

a)   How can this be done without endangering the workers?

....

d)   Gamma radiation can pass easily through the walls of buildings.
How can workers in the surrounding areas be protected from this hazard?

....

Top Tips: You should always handle radioactive sources really carefully. People who work
with radioisotopes often wear **dosimeters** — badges which record their exposure. We're all exposed
to a low level of **background radiation** every day, though — from rocks etc. — and you can't do
anything about that (unless you fancy wearing a lead-lined suit and breathing apparatus all day long.

Risks from Radiation

Q3 Skin cancers are often surgically removed.
Tumours deeper within the body are often treated by radiotherapy, using **gamma rays**.

a) How does radiotherapy treat cancer?

....

b) What properties do gamma rays have which make them suitable for radiotherapy?

....

....

c) Why is a high dose used?

....

Q4 The three different types of radiation can all be dangerous.

a) Which **two** types of radiation can pass through the human body?
Circle the correct answers.

alpha   beta   gamma

b) i) Which type of radiation is usually most dangerous if it's inhaled or swallowed?

....

ii) What effects can this type of radiation have on the human body?

....

Q5 In 1986, a nuclear reactor at Chernobyl (in Ukraine) exploded, and a lot of radioactive material
was released. Many people were exposed to high doses of radiation. Since then scientists have
monitored the health of people living in the affected areas.

a) Why have scientists monitored people's health for so long after the explosion?

Think about half-life and dose.

....

....

b) The Chernobyl explosion provided scientists with a unique opportunity to study
the **effects** of radiation exposure on **humans**. Why could scientists not study this
by collecting data in a laboratory?

....

....

The Origin of the Universe

Q1   Complete this passage using the words supplied below.

| expansion | matter | energy | expand | age | explosion |

Many scientists believe that the Universe started with all the

.... and .... in one small space.

There was a huge .... and the material started to

.... Scientists can estimate the .... of

the Universe using the current rate of ....

Q2   Brian set up a microphone at his local railway station to record his favourite **train noises**. He attached the microphone to an oscilloscope.

An express train passed through the station at a constant speed. Diagram A below shows the trace on the monitor at 11:31:07, as the train **approached** Brian's microphone.

On diagram B, sketch the trace Brian might have seen as the train **left** the station.

A   11:31:07

B   11:31:08

Q3   What **evidence** is there to support the idea that the Universe is expanding? Include a brief explanation of **red-shift** in your answer.

....

....

....

....

Q4   The expanding Universe can be likened to the surface of a bubble which is getting bigger.

a)   What happens to two "particles" which start off near each other as the bubble expands?

....

b)   Some of the material in the Universe actually comes together in galaxies. How can this be explained?

....

....

Looking into Space

Q1 Astronomers can use a number of strategies to improve the quality of the images they get of space from Earth-based telescopes.

a) How can they get good images of **faint**, **distant** objects using optical telescopes?

....

....

....

b) How can they improve an optical telescope's **resolution** (ability to see detail)?

....

....

Q2 The **Hubble Space Telescope** can produce images which are much better than those from any Earth-based optical telescopes of a similar size.

a) Explain why the pictures from the Hubble Telescope are clearer and brighter.

....

....

b) List **three** possible **disadvantages** of using space telescopes.

1. ....

2. ....

3. ....

Q3 Astronomers use various telescopes designed to collect different types of electromagnetic waves. Why do they not just use **optical telescopes** situated on Earth or in space?

....

....

....

Looking into Space

Q4 **Radio telescopes** need to be very large, or else the images are 'fuzzy' and lack detail.

a) Why is this?

....

....

....

b) To produce images with a similar degree of detail, which would need to be **larger** — an infrared telescope or an ultraviolet telescope? Circle the correct answer.

infrared   ultraviolet

Q5 Astronomers can't use X-ray telescopes on Earth.

Explain why this is.

....

....

Q6 Only **one** of these statements about the Hubble Space Telescope is **true**.

Circle A, B, C or D to indicate which statement is correct.

A   It was placed in space in order to get closer to the stars.

B   It is placed in space to avoid problems caused by the atmosphere.

C   It uses radio waves rather than light waves to get a better picture of the stars.

D   It was placed in space so that NASA could use it to spy on Russia.

Top Tips: With telescopes, the rule seems to be 'big is beautiful'. And it's best to think up a good name to make sure everyone knows your telescope's the biggest. There's one in Chile called the Very Large Telescope. Imaginative. Better still, there are plans to build a really big new optical telescope — 100 m across — and call it the Overwhelmingly Large Telescope. Beat that.

Mixed Questions — Physics 1b

Q1 The waves A, B and C represent **infrared**, **visible light** and **ultraviolet** radiation (not in that order).

Tick the box next to any of the following statements which are **true**.

☐ B represents ultraviolet radiation.

☐ The infrared wave has the largest amplitude.

☐ C has the highest frequency.

☐ A has the shortest wavelength.

A

B

C

Q2 Radio Roary transmits **long-wave** signals with a wavelength of **1.5 km**.

a) Calculate the **frequency** of Radio Roary's transmission. (Use speed = 3×10^8 m/s.)

....

....

b) Mr Potts is on holiday in the Scottish Highlands. He follows England's progress in the cricket test match on Radio Roary, but he can't watch the coverage on television, because TV reception at the cottage is so poor.

Explain why Mr Potts gets **good** long-wave radio reception, but such **poor** TV reception.

....

....

c) Radio Piracy broadcasts at a frequency of 201 kHz.
Both Radio Roary and Radio Piracy broadcast **analogue** signals.

i) Why might this be a problem for people listening to these stations?

....

....

ii) Suggest a way to reduce the problem without changing the frequency of the transmissions.

....

Q3 My landline telephone is connected to the telephone exchange by **optical fibres**.

a) What **type** of EM wave might be sent from the exchange? ....

b) Draw an annotated diagram to show how an optical fibre works.

Mixed Questions — Physics 1b

Q4 Remote-sensing **satellites** can be used to 'see' the Earth from space.
Telescopes can be put in space and used to 'see' other parts of the Universe.

a) Many satellites use microwaves to 'see' the Earth. How are these microwaves different from the microwaves used in ovens, and why is this important?

....

....

b) i) In what ways are space telescopes better than Earth-based ones?

....

ii) Some types of telescope will **only** work from space. What kind, and why?

....

Q5 Infrared radiation is used by TV **remote controls**. Jake shows Peter that he can change the TV channel by pointing the remote control at a mirror on the opposite wall.

a) What property of EM rays has Jake demonstrated? Circle the correct answer.

    reflection   refraction   diffraction

b) Peter places a dull black piece of card over the mirror and tries to change channel in the same way. Explain what will happen now and why.

....

....

Q6 Cancer is sometimes treated using **gamma rays**.

a) When any substance **absorbs** EM radiation, what two effects can happen?

....

b) Explain why patients treated with **gamma** rays can feel very ill.

....

c) Cancer can be **caused** as well as treated by exposure to EM radiation.

i) Which types of EM radiation are known to cause cancer?

....

ii) State and explain the link between the frequency of EM radiation and how dangerous it is.

....

....

Mixed Questions — Physics 1b

Q7 The table gives information about four different **radioisotopes**.

Source	Type of Radiation	Half-life
radon-222	alpha	3.8 days
technetium-99m	gamma	6 hours
americium-241	alpha	432 years
cobalt-60	beta and gamma	5.27 years

a) Explain how the atomic structure of cobalt-60 is different from the structure of 'normal' cobalt-59.

....

b) Which sources in the table would be most suitable for each of the uses below?

medical tracers   smoke detectors   detecting leaks in pipes

....

c) Jim measures the count rate of a sample of americium-241 as 120 cpm.
Roughly how long would it take for the count rate to fall below **4 cpm**? Show your working.

....

....

d) Explain how nuclear radiation can cause **ionisation**.

....

....

Q8 The diagram represents a **light wave** emitted by a distant galaxy.

a) On the diagram, redraw the wave to show how it might appear to us on Earth because the light is **red-shifted**.

b) Explain how red-shifts from distant and nearer galaxies provide evidence for the Big Bang theory.

....

....

....

Q9 Why do astronomers often want to make telescopes as **big** as possible?

....

....

SAHW41

Physics 1b — Radiation and the Universe